# IN HER IMAGE

A C.G. JUNG FOUNDATION BOOK

The C. G. Jung Foundation for Analytical Psychology is dedicated to helping men and women grow in conscious awareness of the psychological realities in themselves and society, find healing and meaning in their lives and greater depth in their relationships, and live in response to their discovered sense of purpose. It welcomes the public to attend its lectures, seminars, films, symposia, and workshops and offers a wide selection of books for sale through its bookstore. The Foundation also publishes *Quadrant,* a semiannual journal, and books on Analytical Psychology and related subjects. For information about Foundation programs or membership, please write to the

C. G. JUNG FOUNDATION
28 EAST 39TH STREET
NEW YORK, NY 10016

# IN HER IMAGE

## The Unhealed Daughter's Search for Her Mother

KATHIE CARLSON

SHAMBHALA
BOSTON & SHAFTESBURY
1989

Shambhala Publications, Inc.
Horticultural Hall
300 Massachusetts Avenue
Boston, Massachusetts 02115

Shambhala Publications, Inc.
The Old School House
The Courtyard, Bell Street
Shaftesbury, Dorset SP7 8BP



9 8 7 6 5 4 3 2 1

First Edition
Printed in the United States of America on acid-free paper
Distributed in the United States by Random House and in Canada by Random House of Canada Ltd.
Distributed in the United Kingdom by Element Books, Ltd.

Library of Congress Cataloging-in-Publication Data
Carlson, Kathie.
In her image: the unhealed daughter's search for her mother/
Kathie Carlson.—1st ed.
p. cm.
Bibliography: p.
ISBN 0-87773-507-7
1. Mothers and daughters. 2. Women—Psychology. 3. Interpersonal conflict. 4. Adult children. I. Title
HQ755.85.C358 1989 89-42623
306.874'3—dc20 CIP

To my "heartmothers"
and
to Rachele, my daughter,
who teaches me still . . .

# CONTENTS

*Acknowledgments* *ix*
*Introduction* *xi*
1. Three Perspectives 1
2. Positive Bonds 12
3. The Binding or Banishing Mother 24
4. Touch in the Mother–Daughter Relationship 38
5. Matrophobia and Its Transformation 49
6. The Unhealed Child: Partial Solutions and Healing Possibilities 61
7. Lifesource: Introduction to the Great Mother 74
8. The Great Mother as Archetypal Dynamic in Personal Experience 93
9. One Woman's Journey 114
*Conclusion* 128
*Notes* 133
*Bibliography* 143
*Index* 147
*Credits* 152

# ACKNOWLEDGMENTS

Without the help and encouragement of many people, this book could not have been written and published, and I would like to acknowledge their contributions and offer them thanks. First of all, I would like to thank, anonymously, the woman who convinced me to write this book. Her care, encouragement, and consistent belief in me have sustained me through all the ups and downs. My own experiences as a therapist, teacher, mother, and daughter have been greatly enriched and instructed by the experiences of women friends, students, and clients in therapy. I am especially grateful to those women who have given me permission to use disguised versions of their stories in this book.

Several people read the manuscript in various stages and offered commentary. I'd like to thank Sylvia Perera, Annmari Ronnberg, Maryann Sherby, and Dr. Gertrud Ujhely. Special thanks to Maryann for her editing help and to Gertrud for reading the manuscript in somewhat rushed circumstances. Thanks also to Bezo Morton and her husband, Bob, whose knowledge of books and publishing, general encouragement, and a typewriter rushed to my house when my own died an untimely death were especially helpful to me.

To my family, both "adopted" and biological, I offer deepest thanks for their tolerance and support: to my son, Jake, who began referring to me as a "writer" long before I believed it myself; to my daughter, Rachele, who suffered through many entreaties of "Wait! Don't go out yet; I just want to read you one more page!"; to Mr. and Mrs. Arthur R. French, Jr., my landlord and landlady and "surrogate parents," whose kindness, warmth, and practical help have nurtured both my children and myself for the past several years; and to all my friends both here in the East and in Michigan, on whose love and caring I really depend.

The C.G. Jung Foundation of New York has been an important resource in my life for many years, and I am very grateful for its support of this book. I am grateful to all of the people on the staff of the Foundation who gave various kinds of assistance, but my deepest thanks are to Aryeh Maidenbaum, the Foundation director, whose friendship and enthusiasm for my work have benefited me since I first moved East several years ago.

To the staff at Shambhala Publications, who initiated this neophyte into the labyrinthine ways of book publishing with flexibility, patience, and humor, I offer heartfelt thanks. I am especially grateful to my editor, Emily Hilburn Sell, whose enthusiasm and belief in this book as well as practical help have sustained me from the beginning. My first contact with Emily was especially touching and will be indelible among my experiences as a writer. Responding to Emily's initial call, I reached her at home, and for the next half-hour we negotiated the terms of the book contract to the music of her nursing baby smacking loudly in the background. With such an auspicious, "feminine" beginning, I knew this book couldn't help but succeed.

Finally, I want to acknowledge the spiritual source of all of my work and my life. This book pays homage to Her: Lady, Holy One, Mother of All.

# INTRODUCTION

The primary relationship between women is the relationship of mother and daughter. This relationship is the birthplace of a woman's ego identity, her sense of security in the world, her feelings about herself, her body, and other women. From her mother, a woman receives her first impression of how to be a woman and what being a woman means. She also receives her first access to at least some aspects of the archetypal mother, the Great Mother, and to an experience of the feminine Self. This latter dimension is generally not recognized in our culture.

As a therapist, teacher, mother, and daughter myself, I have been most concerned with the amount of woundedness so many women feel vis-à-vis their mothers, how much "unfinished business" seems to permeate this relationship. I have also been deeply impressed both in myself and in others by the ferociousness and tenacity of longing for "something more." We long for a mother who can give us all that we need from her and receive all that we want to give her. We long to be able to love her and to see ourselves loved in her eyes. We long to be known, to be seen in our deepest selves and liked for who we are by this woman who is our earthly origin and most often our primary caretaker. It is almost impossible to let her go completely, even when the relationship has been and continues to be abusive or fruitless, or when our differences make a chasm too wide to be bridged. Even women who have broken off relationship with their mothers still long for them and continue to wish that there were some way that a true connection could be made. We came from them. We were raised by them. We yearn for a bond.

The persistence of this longing (along with the hurt, anger, and needs related to our mothers that so many of us continue to feel as adults—what Adrienne Rich has so aptly named the "unhealed child" within us[1]) is also the seat of a deeper hunger. The hunger of the unhealed daughter has a collective, archetypal core. Most deeply and broadly, what we long for is a fuller vision of Woman, a vision that can mother our hearts and our souls into their truest being. We need such a Mother but she cannot be located in one human being only. She is bigger than human and greater than the shoulders of the one woman in our lives who has been asked to carry her.

In this book, I want to reconnect the very human problems between mothers and daughters with their deeper psychic roots. This attempt is unique in the literature, for it articulates not only many of the strengths and problems of the mother–daughter relationship but also sets them within a transpersonal context and sees them as part of an individual and collective inner journey. The problems, woundings, strengths, and delights of the mother–daughter relationship are also part of a deep spiritual search among women, a search for a more authentic feminine Sourceground for their lives. This search may be unconscious, peeking through unresolved human longings and conflicts or mirrored in individual visions and dreams. Or it may be part of the expanding collective consciousness, as is reflected in the Women's Movement, the proliferation of literature in feminine psychology, and the emergence of women's spirituality particularly during the past decade.

Much of the framework of this book was developed initially for teaching classes on the mother–daughter relationship to adult women. These classes were usually eight weeks in length and were taught either privately or as part of the public adult education programs of various Jungian or transpersonally oriented organizations. The classes were usually didactic as well as experiential, including weekly reading in the literature on mothers and daughters as well as discussion and exchange of personal experiences. In most of the nonacademic classes I have taught, in addition to a classroom forum for exchange and sharing, I have tried to provide an introverted focus for the material by offering each woman the option of keeping a private journal for the duration of the class. This journal centered on "focus questions" I would hand out each week, aimed at helping her focus her own personal experience with the topic at hand. This was especially helpful for women who had difficulty articulating their personal experiences or who were more at home with a more introverted process than the classroom provided. These journals were not shared in class, although some women drew from them personally to illustrate points made by me or others in the class.

*In Her Image* goes significantly beyond what I taught in class, particularly in its expansion of material on the Goddess and in its inclusion of dreams, fantasy, and other therapeutic material. Stories from friends, workshop participants, women in therapy, and my own experiences as mother, daughter, and granddaughter have been added to personal examples of my students. Ultimately, in writing the book, I hoped to expand and deepen the material while still maintaining the broad base and accessibility that I strive for as a teacher.

Most of this book is written from the viewpoint of the daughter, the common thread among women, since all women are daughters of mothers. However, much of this book is directly relevant to mothers and mothering as well. Three perspectives, each of which I consider vital to a whole view of the mother, inform this book throughout: the child's view, which preserves the daughter's centrality and her need for her mother; the feminist view, which seeks to take into account the effects of the collective environment on the mother–daughter relationship; and a transpersonal view of the mother, which sets human mothering within its archetypal background of the Great Mother. Ultimately, this book is addressed to the unhealed daughter in us all, to help her better comprehend what she *has* experienced within its broader and deeper context, and to enable her to seek out more effectively what she *hasn't* experienced and needs for the fulfillment of her soul.

# 1

# THREE PERSPECTIVES

Several perspectives are necessary to gain a full vision of the mother–daughter relationship. The perspectives I have found to be most helpful in teaching and doing therapy with women are those centered in a child, a feminist, and a transpersonal point of view. These three perspectives articulate successively broader and deeper visionings of the mother. Each one has its merits and limitations and each is vital to the daughter's comprehension of her inner and outer experience of her mother.

In the first vision, the daughter sees her mother through the eyes of a child, and through the dependency dynamics that existed in her early relationship with her mother. Most women see their mothers through this perspective at some level, even if through subsequent learning and reflection they have acquired a more adult viewpoint that takes a larger picture into account.

The daughter who is looking through a child's eyes makes several assumptions about her mother. First, she assumes that her mother is really powerful or could be if she wanted to be. Secondly, she believes that her mother has control over her life because she is an adult. Even a woman who has learned to see the personal and collective factors that shaped her mother's parenting style and capacity may go back to this earlier view when thinking about her own childhood. Thus, one of the college students I worked with in therapy, a gifted, mature young woman, who got along well with both of her parents and was particularly empathic with her mother, was baffled at her mother's newly emerged resentment at "never having done what I wanted to do in life." She told me that it seemed to her that her mother always did *exactly* what she wanted to do. Further reflection on her reactions led her to realize that a part of her was hurt and frightened by her mother's statement and wanted to maintain the belief that her mother had always had the power to do whatever she wanted. If the full-time mothering that the mother had done was not what she wanted to do in life, where did this leave the daughter, particularly since her experience was one of feeling well cared for and loved? The security of her childhood experience was threatened by her mother's revelation, and secretly she feared that if her mother resented having been a full-time mother, she must resent her daughter as well. Maintaining the image of her mother as all-powerful also preserved a sense of her child self as having deserved the care she had been given.

The child's view is egocentric; it evaluates the mother in terms of how her behavior affected the child, how the daughter's needs and longings were met or not met. All positive experience is seen as good and "right," and there is a truth in that, for it *was* right for the child. All negative experience (e.g., the mother's absence, preoccupations, or angers) is perceived as aimed at the daughter and personally motivated even when this is obviously not the case (as, for example, when a mother is absent because she is hospitalized due to mental or physical illness). In addition, the child view believes that it was (and is) possible for all the daughter's legitimate needs to have been met by the mother "if only—." Many an adult daughter has a whole list of "if onlys" to bolster her child belief that the mother could give her most or all of what she needs. "If only I had been a better daughter"; "if only she hadn't gone to work full-time"; "if only she would stop lecturing me"; "if only she were less concerned with appearances. . . ." And the final clause to all of these "if onlys" is: "*then* she would be the mother I wanted" or "*then* we could finally have a relationship."

The child's perspective, on the one hand, is the outgrowth of taking seriously and valuing the *true* needs of the child, needs that are legitimate and vital for us to be aware of even as adults. Valuing these needs and this part of ourselves contributes to a healthy ego and to a sense of wholeness and self-worth as an adult; women who suppress or deny their child perspectives lose a vital part of themselves. Such women are often unable to care well for themselves or to receive care from others. On the other hand, the child perspective on the mother is steeped in the dependency dynamics inherent in patriarchal child-rearing arrangements in which the mother tends to be the sole caretaker of the child or is expected to be and is therefore seen consensually as the "all-fulfiller."[1] (We tend to let up on grandmothers, aunts, and even fathers, who may have played vital roles in our lives but were not expected to be emotionally responsible for all of our needs.) Thus, this perspective is also supported by cultural stereotypes and expectations of what the mother can and is supposed to be: supportive, nurturing, unselfish, infinitely caring of the child, etc.

The problem is that *no one* can be all that; the expectations placed on mothers are inhuman, yet we've had nowhere else to refer them. A man who has been disappointed or hurt in relationship with his personal father can sometimes find his way to a "heavenly" Father, a God image that can carry the greater-than-human expectations. As daughters in a culture that offers no feminine God image, we've had no place else to turn.

Many of us have not had even adequate mothering, much less the ideal; many of our mothers have been too depleted themselves. We end up disappointed in our mothers, hurt, angry, blaming, needy, raging, yet unable to let go of our need for them. We feel starved emotionally and try to cover that over. We feel terrified of becoming like our mothers and vow to be different with our children. We end up estranged from our mothers and estranged from ourselves. We carry around an unhealed child, a sense of woundedness and of longing that seems to have nowhere to go. Identifying with this child in ourselves, expanding her vision, and connecting her with healing possibilities are the underlying themes of this book.

The child's view of the mother–daughter relationship is both valuable and limited. It is valuable because it allows preservation of legitimate needs for attention, nurturance, care, and primary bonding; these needs are true even for the adult and should not be dismissed. Also preserved by this perspective is a sense of oneself as important and central, a birthright not easily claimed by women in a culture that has so often exhorted them to put others first. The child's position counters and compensates both personal and cultural experiences of the devaluation and psychological "decentralization" of women and focuses attention on the self. Even the rage and blaming that often emerge when the unhealed child comes into consciousness may be necessary, not as an end point (and unfortunately, many daughters get stuck here), but as a way of separating out and claiming oneself vis-à-vis one's mother, and as a basis for legitimate self-interest and self-assertion. All of this focus on oneself and assertion of one's true needs are necessary to sustain a healthy ego that can feed and maintain the adult woman.

At the same time, the child's viewpoint is limited. It does not see the mother in herself, as a person with her own needs, interests, and concerns separate from the child. Nor does it take into account important factors affecting the mother's life and ability to parent, factors such as economics, what kinds of supports the mother herself had available, what her own experience of being mothered was. It also overlooks the effects that cultural expectations and stereotypes of mothers have on the mother's parenting (e.g., she may be living a false self because she's doing what she thinks she's "supposed" to do). And finally, the child's perspective envisions the mother inhumanly, assumes she is somehow "matched" to the daughter's needs, does not have needs of her own that conflict with her daughter's, and has nearly infinitely resources.

A second perspective—seeing our mothers through feminist eyes—expands the child's vision. This extremely valuable and necessary viewpoint is an adult perspective rooted in a different power dynamic than that of the child's. From this vantage, the mother is seen as an equal, a "sister," a woman like oneself. In addition, an attempt is made to separate out the cultural image of "mother" and the institution of motherhood from this particular human being.[2] Cultural and environmental factors are taken into account and the mother's parenting is seen as a response to these factors as well as being the creation of her own personality and abilities. Remembering her mother's literal or emotional absence, for example, which she may have felt keenly as a child, the daughter is now able to take into account a broader picture of the mother's life. She may understand, as an adult, the economic pressure that necessitated that her mother work long hours away from home. She may recognize the submission to a collective ideal that may have led her mother to have had more children than she had time and energy for. She may also come to realize that some of her mother's pattern of mothering was a replica of her grandmother's and that both women's styles were in part a reflection of the culture, which has an investment in reproducing itself and its values in the socialization process mothers are expected to undertake with regard to their children (i.e., the preparation for and induction into the society's values).[3]

Many a mother has gone against her own instincts and preferences in deference to the so-called "experts" because she genuinely wanted to raise her child "right" and was not expected to be able to determine what was right from her own instinct or authority. I still remember the time when my daughter was very little and had great difficulty sleeping whenever she was sick. I'd be up and down all night with her, growing progressively more irritable and exhausted as the night wore on. I thought of taking her into bed with me, which seemed the natural thing to do, but recalled Dr. Spock's admonition against this, his warning about what a bad habit would be formed as a consequence. Unsure of myself as a parent, reasoning that I didn't "know" anything about children since I had been an only child myself, I followed his dictum. (It never occurred to me to question whether Spock himself had ever been up all night with a sick baby and had a two-year-old as well to cope with in the morning.) Finally one night I could barely function and put Rachele next to me in bed, just so I could lie down. Comforted by my presence and by being close to my body, she immediately went to sleep and, though still ill, continued to sleep through the night.

The feminist perspective is valuable because it allows the daughter to extend an empathic concern to her mother, seeing her as a limited adult instead of an ideal. It takes into account multiple cultural and environmental, as well as personal, factors that affect her mothering. The feminist view has also given weight and value to women who have served as "counter-mothers"[4] in the daughter's life: grandmothers, aunts, nannies, teachers, and other women who have provided an adjunct or alternative care to the mother's. The presence of such women in our lives allows the needs of the unhealed child to be spread out among many "mothers" and addressed by several different sources of care. One woman in one of my mother–daughter classes whose mother had often been mentally ill while she was growing up suddenly realized how much nurturing one of her aunts had provided; she had never thought of this as "mothering" before and immediately got in touch with her aunt to thank her.

The limit of this perspective lies in the possibility that other truly personal factors in the mother–daughter relationship that are not caused by the environment may be overlooked, factors such as differences in temperament or psychological type (e.g., problems of the extraverted mother raising an introverted daughter or vice versa). In addition, in spite of the fact that feminism has encouraged and facilitated self-care, some women may use their feminist views to split off from the unhealed child within themselves, extending their empathy only toward their mothers and excluding the validity of their own unmet needs.

Sometimes women who have relinquished their child perspective on their experiences with their mothers have to be encouraged to reclaim it, in order to bring up and work through the precious parts of themselves that got locked away when the child self was suppressed. One woman, who had been severely abused by her father with her mother's knowledge, resisted seeing her mother negatively in any way. Her mother was also being abused, she said; they were poor and her mother held down a job to try to support the family when the father wouldn't or was unable to. All of this was admirable on the part of the mother and, from my patient's strong feminist perspective, an empathic vision of the forces her mother struggled to contend with. What was missing from this picture was the same kind of empathy for herself, empathy for the unmothered and abused child, feeling for her own needs and pain as deeply as she felt for her mother's.

It is not necessary to denigrate one's mother to hold many points of view simultaneously, even when the foci inherent in these points of view clash. It is possible to learn to have deep compassion, concern, and even outrage on behalf of the child one was, regardless of how legitimate or inevitable the factors were that led to abusive or neglectful behavior.[5] The child's passion and egocentrism don't care about what is going on with the mother in her own life and shouldn't be asked to; her rage at being mistreated or having her needs unmet should be valued as part of her claiming her importance in the world, her intrinsic worth as a human being. When a woman holds down or denies these feelings, a great deal else is lost: an intrinsic sense of self-worth, an ability to identify what in the environment or in other people is dangerous to her and to respond with self-protection, and much of the child's spontaneity and passionate interest in herself. A person who has suppressed her child's needs and viewpoint will find it almost impossible to adequately care for herself or to care about herself. Her perceptiveness and empathic concern for others may be extremely well developed; she may be a fine caretaker of everyone except herself. Championing her mother's worth at the expense of her own reflects exactly what was true in the first place: that there is no adequate *mother* in the situation. There was not in the past, and is not internally in the present. The person who has suppressed her child self and cannot stand for her own experience grows into an adult who must continue to be unmothered, who cannot take in support and love from others because she cannot claim her right to have them or to have had these things in the past.

Seeing only through a feminist view skews the picture. What was missing from my patient's tale were other aspects of her mother's behavior. The mother made no attempt to stop the father from beating and raping his daughter; and, in addition, when the daughter tried to intervene in her mother's beatings, the mother would turn against her and join the father in beating the daughter. No one can dismiss the pressures in this mother's life which underlay her inability to be empathic and protective of her daughter; yet to fail to feel alarm and concern for the battered child is to collude in dismissing her own legitimate needs for more of a mothering presence than she could manage for herself.

While a woman who has only the child's point of view of her mother may need to add a feminist view in order to expand her picture and understanding of her mother, a woman who claims only a feminist view may need to find or reclaim the child's. I am not trying to set these views against each other, only to point out that *both* are necessary to work toward a whole picture in which both mother and daughter are adequately seen and valued but neither at the expense of the other. Holding both views simultaneously involves a certain level of tension, since it is quite hard (and, from a therapeutic perspective, not necessarily useful) to feel compassion for another and outrage on one's own behalf at the same time. In experiences less extreme than the example given, it may be possible to take both viewpoints into account at the same time. At any rate, both are vital if one is not to lose some very precious aspects of the daughter's reality.[6]

A third view of the mother–daughter relationship revisions

mother and daughter from a transpersonal orientation. In this perspective, the child's needs are taken very seriously and seen and carried as legitimate, but no longer put on the personal mother alone. They are also referred to the transpersonal level, to the spiritual entity of the Great Mother, as She manifests Her various aspects in other human beings and appears in both ancient and modern visions and dreams. This perspective adds to and extends the feminist awareness that there are other resources available and that "mother" is bigger than personal experience with one woman. If we have other sources to turn to and our needs are not devalued, it is easier to put our personal mothers in perspective; we can accept their limits more easily because we have more than "one chance."

The transpersonal perspective also allows us to revision the cultural stereotype of "mother" and to preserve it, not as a realistic ideal that one human being should be expected to live up to, but as part of a vision of the Feminine as Deity that has existed for thousands of years and is part of our inner and outer heritage. The woman who is infinitely supportive, nurturing, unselfish, and caring, who can feed others without needing to feed herself—the image of that great an abundance—is an archetypal image. It resides in the deepest and most collective layers of the psyche and found its most vivid expression in the imagery of prepatriarchal religions, thousands of years ago.

The mistake that we make as a culture is to expect one human woman to *be* the archetype and, further, to be only that aspect of the mother archetype we want, that we see as positive. The cultural stereotype of the "good mother" is but one part of a much larger entity; the archetype is more complicated and bi-valent than we would choose. The Great Mother has both a benevolent and a terrible side, and either or both may come through our personal mothers as well as through ourselves and other women. We don't get to choose and, to a very real extent, neither do our mothers. A woman can't *make* herself into the good archetypal mother simply by willing herself to be it, no matter how hard she tries. The fact that women are expected to do this, to have this power, is one of the major problems in human relationships today, and differentiating themselves from such expectations poses a central individuation task for modern women. To know that one carries the archetype and can relate to it but not control it—and to know that one is also *not* the archetype, not that powerful or full or unlimited—is the cultural lesson that mothers and daughters alike need to learn.

What we can choose to do is to *relate* to the archetypal Mother in a conscious, voluntary way, to get in touch with a heritage of spiritual vision that belongs to all of us but that has been stamped out of our collective awareness by the destructive aspects of patriarchal culture. Contacting this heritage enables us to reconnect with a time, uninfluenced by patriarchal views of women, when "feminine" was experienced as vast, multifaceted, and valuable—so valuable that it appeared as a God image. Whether we look at this heritage and its reappearance in modern times as a history we can draw from for images and inspiration, as the mirror of forces within and between us, or as a spiritual image—a living Goddess whose children we are—we can, by connecting with this perspective, come to see our mothers and ourselves differently. We can come to see what of the Great Mother came through our personal mother experiences, what of Her radiance and Her terror, and raise questions of deeper meaning. Further, we can seek out aspects we haven't experienced that we need for healing and for wholeness. Through this vision, we can eventually become daughters of ourselves, of each other, and of a Mother as vast as our vision can stretch. It is true that in the process, something will also be lost; our personal mothers can no longer carry the "bigness" we've attributed to them, or be expected to be the only carrier of the Mother our bodies and souls need; but, in exchange, we can gain all the richness of the transpersonal world.

Knowledge of the Great Mother's images and stories provides pictures, models, and connections across time and culture to female sources and to a multiplicity of "styles" of being female. Through meditation, imaginal play, art, and worship, the Great Mother can give us what our personal mothers often could not.

Each perspective depicted in this chapter gives us access to the mother. The childhood perspective gives us each a personal connection to one human being as mother. The feminist perspective relates us to other women in our culture and puts our mothers in cultural context. The transpersonal perspective expands this to include connection with a spiritual source and people across time.

To summarize: The child perspective sees the mother egocentrically, believing her to be all-powerful and able to fulfill the daughter's needs. The mother is not seen as individual, or as limited by circumstances within and without. The great expectations surrounding her from this perspective are rarely met; this gives rise to the unhealed child full of rage, blame, hurt, and need. Although frustrating and too narrow, the unhealed child is a true inner experience; it is valuable for finding and claiming the importance of oneself. The feminist perspective places the mother in a social and cultural context, and takes into account both her personal difficulties and the environmental impact on her. The feminist perspective may lead to an objective understanding of the mother as a limited human being, but risks losing connection with the unhealed child. The transpersonal perspective sees both mother and daughter against the backdrop of a rich spiritual heritage. The mother is no longer asked to carry the archetype alone; resources are found in other women, history, and spiritual connections.

All three of these perspectives minister to our need for wholeness. The child and feminist perspectives will dominate the next five chapters, which explore the personal experience of the mother, factors affecting her life, and the unhealed child. This exploration leads into the revisioning, healing possibilities and the transpersonal focus of the subsequent three chapters.

# 2

# POSITIVE BONDS

The smell of Lipton tea can still conjure my grandmother's presence. I remember her smells, the way her dresses felt to my touch, the heavy stockings and shoes she wore. It was she who did the cooking and cleaning, she who tended the plants and animals. I remember eating the apple peels as she prepared the apples for pie, making my own little cookies out of scraps of the dough, recall the names of foods from her Austro-Hungarian background: butterhorns, tuvitch, Äpfel in Schlafrock. My parents saw her as a fussy perfectionist, insistent on cleanliness and order; I remember her clothes, face, glasses spattered with tomatoes as she immersed herself in the annual canning, her hands and knees dirt-encrusted from working in the garden.

My gramma was my primary mother, not just because she was present more often than my working mother and did most of the child care but because, in contrast to my mother who was distant, rejecting, and often emotionally abusive, my grandmother let me into her life and participated in mine. I liked to sit on her bed in the mornings and watch her deftly work her long, thin hair into the knot she wore at the back of her neck. It was she who allowed me to ponder with frank curiosity her aging, naked body while my mother recoiled with horror the one time I, realizing my breasts were going to grow, excitedly asked if I could see hers to know what mine would look like. I remember my grandmother's hands, how the veins stood out on the back of them; she told me that that was a sign of hard work and for years I despaired over my own smooth hands because I, too, wanted to be a hard-working woman. When I was desperately lonely and longed for a brother or sister, she bought me a dog. When I went through a period of being very worried about illness, she gave me a necklace of salmon-colored beads; the beads, she said, would turn pale whenever I was getting sick. I watched the beads carefully, believed in their consistently robust color, and grew past my anxiety on the strength of my grandmother's magic.

Her garden was her passion; only there was she free of the melancholy that engulfed her when she realized she was just the "caretaker" in my parents' house, only there was she really herself, silently absorbed and free. From her I learned a wordless drinking in of ecstatic, sensual beauty: color, perfume, exquisite and intricate form. Recently I realized that my own deep connection with nature, which engendered and defined my spiritual life as a child, has its origins in her respect and reverence for her garden.

My grandmother framed the world of my childhood; food, body, faith and magic, sensuality, all of these belonged to her as well as the larger and more mysterious world of nature. I lived by her rhythms, her rules, her generosities, and limits. This existence was not ideal. She was in her sixties when I was born; I was always aware at some level that raising yet another child at this point in her life was too much for her. She could not tolerate, for example, the presence of other children; her sense of being responsible for them as well as for me made her nervous and controlling, though even here she made an effort sometimes to get past her difficulties when she perceived my longing and my loneliness.

The strength and depth of our positive bonding was cut short forever by the untreated psychosis that erupted in my grandmother when I was in my early teens and savaged us both, sending her into delusional isolation and me into psychology books. For many years after, even in therapy, I remembered almost nothing of my grandmother's presence in my life; memory was locked in unspeakable grief and loss, some of which I am still unable to recover. But recently, the sweetness of the early times rushes back to me, unfolds itself in sensate, feeling memory, and I find that it matters to me deeply to remember how she loved me, to see myself through her eyes as someone dear and worth loving, and to realize on an emotional level what I only knew intellectually before: that the paranoid attacks and accusations she hurled at me (and at others) in my teens did not represent her true feeling toward me and would never have been intended had she stayed sane. Historically, our positive bond dissolved in her descent into madness, from which she was never to recover, but I am coming to realize that love's imprint is never destroyed, not by psychosis or even by death.

Most women have had some positive experience with their mothers or mother figures, even if fleeting or short lived. Some women refute this experience as they get older and learn to measure their mothers by the cultural ideal; others cannot claim these experiences because the other, more problematical aspects of the relationship are too painful and predominate. For many women, however, the positive bond that existed, at least at times, with their mothers becomes an ongoing source of inner security and self-nourishment.

This experience is vividly illustrated on a child's level in a poem of Anne Sexton's:

Oh Mother,
here in your lap,
as good as a bowlful of clouds,
I your greedy child
am given your breast,
the sea wrapped in skin,
and your arms,
roots covered with moss
and with new shoots sticking out
to tickle the laugh out of me.
Yes, I am wedded to my teddy
but he has the smell of you
as well as the smell of me.
Your necklace that I finger
is all angel eyes.
Your rings that sparkle

are like the moon on the pond.
Your legs that bounce me up and down,
your dear nylon-covered legs,
are the horses I will ride
into eternity.
Oh Mother,
after this lap of childhood,
I will never go forth
into the big people's world
as an alien,
a fabrication,
or falter
   when someone else
is as empty as a shoe.[1]

Sexton's poem mirrors a child's attachment to her mother in which world and mother are initially fused, but anticipates an ongoing connection between mother and world once the separation has been made. A solid, positive bond with her mother creates a base from which the daughter can go forth into the larger world beyond her mother, carrying with her the sense of security and belonging first experienced in the mother–daughter relationship. Moving out into the world, the daughter's ego bears the imprint and valance of her first "home." (This, of course, is also true of negative experience of her mother.)

As adults, we also need an inner security that serves as a base from which to go out into the world. Many of us depend on family ties, the support of friends, or deeply held religious beliefs to provide something we can return to again and again for comfort, encouragement, and a sense of belonging to something bigger than ourselves. For some adult daughters, an ongoing positive connection with their mothers serves as a feminine wellspring for the sustenance of their adult lives, providing a continuity with the past and an inspiration in the present. Crystal Eastman, one of the founders of the ACLU, expressed this movingly in a letter written to her mother, Annis:

Dearest,

The laundry has just come—Wednesday at noon. However, the things are all right. The cake was in time for my dessert, and I do think it is the best you ever made.

Oh, you will never know just what it meant to me to have it come today! I have been feeling lately somewhat lost and stranded, as if I couldn't tell where or with what people I belonged. You know, as you go along, you keep discovering weaknesses in the people, or the movements, or places, that you were once altogether in sympathy with. Your thought turns from one stronghold to another, and it seems to be the same with all. On top of it, perhaps even causing it all, is a sense of your *own* miserable inefficiency. Well, after awhile you keep saying to yourself, almost subconsciously, "where—with whom can I cast my lot—and feel that my whole heart and soul is in the throw?" This in a poor way describes my state of mind since Sunday. Perhaps you are wondering what this has to do with the laundry? Can't you see? It came as a visible sign of *you*, of your realness, your work, and thought, and love. And suddenly I knew that I belong to *you*. My lonely spirit was comforted; the world no longer seemed an empty place.

It is so clear to me, every little while, that my soul is not big enough to get along without a very personal reason for existence. You will be the person for a long, long time yet. Won't you?

Well, this is only one of the inevitable "downs" that come to an ambitious person like me. I shall soon brace up and find my place again. And you must forget that I am ever blue, remembering only that when I am, the thought of you, or a letter or package from you can almost always pull me out.[2]

Annis Eastman was a gifted speaker, organizer, and homemaker, active in the women's suffrage movement; her daughter was an equally accomplished social activist. As evinced by this letter, written when Crystal Eastman was in her twenties, their relationship as adults was as passionate and extraordinary as their individual lives, full of intense love, interest, and support for each other's activities.[3]

The psychic imprint of a positive mother can continue to nourish her daughter even after the mother has died. This was vividly described by a woman in one of my classes. Janet had always been a mischievous child. Lively and into everything, she was always being punished by her strict father. Her mother, however, would support her daughter each time and soften or undo the father's punishments. Janet particularly remembered a time when she had been sent to her room by her father for some misdemeanor or another and was sitting on her bed, hurt and crying at the felt injustice of her father's anger. Suddenly she heard her mother's footsteps coming up the walk. "As soon as I heard her footsteps," Janet recalled, "I knew that whatever happened, it would be all right." Janet's mother died when Janet was twenty years old; mother and daughter had been particularly close and now, in her thirties, Janet still missed her keenly. But her mother's influence lives on. As she was telling the story of her early bond with her mother to my class, she suddenly remembered something that had happened when she was giving birth to her first child, several years after her mother's death. After many hours of labor, the baby was about to be born; alone and frightened, Janet braced herself against the next round of pain. Suddenly she heard her mother's footsteps in the hospital corridor; she knew then that she would get through this birth and that everything would be all right.

Sometimes concrete objects retain the memory of the good mother and help to maintain her presence in the daughter's life: photographs, pieces of clothing, jewelry, quilts, family heirlooms. For me, it is my grandmother's chopping board which immediately conjures up the image of her hands chopping chives or onions as part of preparation for supper; the whole kitchen comes back to me, its colors, smells, sounds, all permeated with her presence. I remember sitting patiently at the kitchen table, watching her cook, and listening to "One Man's Family" or "Baby Snooks" on the radio or chanting the rhyme she taught me in German (undoubtedly invented at a moment when her patience with a lively and talkative little girl was wearing thin) about a mother who is cooking spinach and bacon and "the little one has to go away, away, away." A woman in one of my classes, when asked to recount a positive story about her mother, remembered how every night when she was a child, her mother would get her and her sister up to go to the bathroom and afterwards, each time, would wrap them both in a blanket and rock them back to sleep. Suddenly she stopped speaking and a look of wonder came over her face. "I still have the blanket," she reported. "I never realized that that might mean something."

Another student of mine, Rebecca, *created* an object that contained and preserved a precious memory of her mother, a vision of her mother's beauty and enjoyment of beautiful clothes. In this case, the daughter's attempt to preserve this aspect of her mother was also an attempt to "repair" a broken image of her since the mother had disowned this part of herself following a mutilating surgery. Before a "botched up mastectomy that made her look like a side of meat," Rebecca reported, her mother had been a vital and active woman with great enjoyment of beautiful clothes. After the surgery, Rebecca tried, repeatedly, to get her mother to reconnect with this part of herself, buying her beautiful dresses and begging her to wear them, but her mother would always look at her body and proclaim, "It's no use." When her mother died and Rebecca and her sister were going through her clothes and other personal things, both were struck by the difference in the dresses she wore before and after her cancer. Rebecca took several dresses from the time before her mother's illness and cut them into patches out of which she made a skirt for herself. In this way she preserved for herself the image of the mother she most wanted to remember, as a model for her own relationship to her body and feminine beauty. This poignant example suggests that the daughter's image of her mother is in part a *process* that can at times create and preserve the aspects of her mother that a daughter most needs, even when the mother herself has "lost" or rejected her own connection to these parts of herself.

In fact, much of the daughter's inner image can be woven around some sense of a mother who's been "lost." This may refer to the mother one once had who went under to illness, depression, overwork, or other changes in the mother's life, as in the case of Rebecca; or to the woman the mother once was before she assumed the roles of wife and mother. Many daughters have heard stories about their mothers before marriage or children that suggest quite a different picture than the women they now experience (both Nancy Friday and Judith Arcana, in their books on mothers and daughters, report personal instances of this yearning for the "lost" mother in this form),[4] women who were once more vital, adventurous, sexual, or independent. Pictures of their mothers as individual women with their own particular temperaments and interests, separate from their wife and mother roles, are compelling for many daughters; the daughter longs to know this woman the mother once was, to call her back to her mother and draw from her spirit and qualities. Sometimes divorce is the point of eclipse for a mother's vitality (though sometimes also its facilitator). Jill was a woman I worked with in therapy who had very little memory of her childhood or early experience of her mother. She vaguely recalled that her mother had been different before her divorce from Jill's father when Jill was eight years old, more related, more vibrant. After the divorce, her mother was constantly ill and not caring of either herself or her child, "like a broken woman," Jill recalled. At one point in our work, Jill brought in some photographs of her family for me to see which included pictures of her mother before and after the divorce. The change that Jill remembered only vaguely was immediately visible in the photos in a startling and graphic way. In the pictures taken before the divorce, the mother appeared as a broadly smiling, friendly looking woman with a strong, open body stance. The pictures after the divorce portrayed a woman so different that it was virtually impossible to see her as being the same person. The woman in the second set of pictures was considerably aged (although the two series of pictures were only a year apart), worn looking, with a body that seemed to have collapsed in on itself. Had I not known ahead of time that this too was Jill's mother, I would never have been able to guess from the visual cues in the pictures. As she remembered more and more of her childhood, Jill longed for connection with that earlier, vital mother she once had, and realized that she was trying to replicate that connection in her current attempts to get nurturing from a man.

Another level of yearning for the lost mother that is prominent in the psychology of adult women is yearning for the mother we never had: a revalued, powerful, strong, positive woman to be connected to and to have come *from*. At bottom, we yearn for our own and our mothers' wholeness and the wholeness of the dismembered Feminine in our culture—which has indeed been "lost" but, like Rebecca's skirt, can be pieced together and recreated. This is a soul task for women today, which both includes and transcends the connection with the personal mother.

A basic ingredient in positive mother–daughter bonding is mutual attachment; this includes both the desire and capacity for intimacy and the allowance of access to each other emotionally and physically. Some women remember this attachment as passionately intense in childhood. One woman spoke of a "lovey time" with her mother when she was very young, a period of play and affection; she remembered much hugging and kissing and nibbling at her mother's earlobes. This would cease abruptly when her father walked into the room. As an adult, she still longed for the quality of acceptance and delight in her relationships that she had experienced in those earliest days. A sense of coming from the mother and belonging to her is a vital part of a positive bond for many women, as mirrored in Anne Sexton's poem and Crystal Eastman's letter. Being allowed to admire her mother and to "participate" in her activities or try on parts of her life and personality is also a component of a daughter's experience of a positive mother.

The mother becomes a role model for her daughter at least at some stages of the daughter's development, extending to the daughter a sense of participation in something bigger and beyond herself. (I remember with amusement how my daughter, having often heard me speak about my career to friends and colleagues, referred to her kindergarten activities as her "work.") Women who have difficulty receiving admiration or allowing themselves to be role models, because they were taught to be self-effacing or feel too inadequate, inadvertently wound their daughters, who begin to feel that their pleasure in their mothers is something bad or unwanted that has no place to go because it is not received. The mother's low self-esteem makes a barrier between her and her daughter, robbing both of a potential channel of mutual nourishment.

In a predominantly positive relationship, the mother creates an emotional and psychological "container" for the child which, like the literal uterus during gestation, has both boundaries and flexibility, growing with the daughter until she is ready to move out of the maternal container into a larger world. Rules, limits, familiar rituals, and endearments define the parameter of this container, while empathic companioning and spontaneity enable it to be flexible and adapted to the child's shifting needs. Consistency is particularly important when it is possible, conveying to the daughter a sense of safety and constancy in being held by her mother. Ruptures of this psychic container can literally disorient the child as in the following example. Jean, who had always shared a warm and close connection with her mother, recalled coming home from kindergarten one day and discovering that her mother wasn't there. Her mother was always home when Jean returned from school, but this day there was no response to her increasingly panicked calls. "It was like the world disappeared and I didn't know where I was," Jean described. Eventually she discovered that her mother was only in the basement out of earshot.

Appropriate protectiveness is also part of a positive bond with the mother. The daughter is not left on her own to cope with situations beyond her capacity but encouraged to lean on her mother's ego while being guided to learn her own skills. When this support is not provided, the daughter often learns to mask her fears and inadequate skills with an air of bravado and pseudocompetence. She may even put herself in danger, either out of ignorance or to test herself repeatedly in an attempt to conquer her fears.

Many women in our culture have not experienced a positive bond with their mothers or have had this bond available only for fleeting moments. Innumerable factors in both the mother's and daughter's lives can interrupt or prevent such a bond.[5] The container may be disrupted by a mother's illness, alcoholism, or mental illness; what becomes all too familiar to the daughter is an erratic atmosphere in which the mother is not available to the child or the routine is continually disrupted. The daughter may not know what to depend on vis-à-vis her mother or what will happen next; her mother may be unavailable to her because of being hospitalized, out of touch with reality, or otherwise debilitated.

Fathers sometimes interfere with the formation or preservation of a positive mother–daughter bond in various ways.[6] The father may be jealous of the bond, wanting either the mother or the daughter all to himself. Either situation is difficult for the daughter, but if she is the one favored by the father, she is placed in an impossible position between her parents. She may be told by her father that she is better, more pleasing, and prettier than her mother and may feel this as positive support from her father. But then she loses connection with her mother because she is set up as her mother's competitor. Conversely, the mother may put the father first, devaluing herself as a mother and shutting out her daughter. Some mothers even bond with their husbands against their daughters or feel compelled to be the instrument of the father's ideas or "programs" for the child.[7] All connection with the daughter takes place via the father or the father's ideas; many a mother–daughter relationship has been sacrificed on the altar of marital "duty."

The mother's relationship to herself may also interfere with or preclude a positive bond with her daughter. If she has had difficulty developing a separate identity of her own, she may need to feed off her daughter for her own sense of self, merging with her instead of containing her. Closeness in this instance becomes a kind of binding, rather than relating, and the seeming support for her daughter is fraudulent and self-serving. The maternal container becomes rigid and fixed and doesn't allow the daughter to go forth beyond it. Or the mother may be unable to facilitate or tolerate intimacy with her daughter, and banish her to a distance. The psychology of these mothers is explored in the next chapter.

# 3

# THE BINDING OR BANISHING MOTHER

> I like to think of my love for my daughter as the "slack net" spread beneath a performing aerialist. I hoped that she would not view with alarm or undue apprehension the necessity for its being there, but rather climb as high as she might care to go, secure in the knowledge of its support. It was frightening to know that pulling the corners too tightly could send her bouncing off into oblivion and leaving the knots too loose might plunge her into certain disaster. . . . What I wanted most for my daughter was that she be able to soar confidently in her own sky, wherever that might be, and if there was space for me as well, I would indeed have reaped what I had tried to sow. —HELEN CLAES[1]

What a woman needs from her mother is an experience of both nurturance and support for autonomy.[2] She needs to know that not only will she be literally taken care of but that her mother can enjoy caretaking. She needs to feel close, not only emotionally but physically, to have access to her mother's body and to feel that her own body is liked and valued by her mother. She needs to be able to bond with her mother, to model after her at least initially, to be able to lean on her mother's ego strengths while she is developing her own. All of this is implied in the positive bonding between mother and daughter that we explored in the last chapter. But what a daughter also needs, in addition to intimacy and closeness, is permission and support to separate from her mother: to accomplish on her own, to make her own mistakes and have her own triumphs, and to be as different from her mother as her own personality and inner patterns direct her to be.

In our culture, many mothers are able to support one side or the other of this delicate balance between closeness and separateness but not both. Some women may have no difficulty forming a close bond with their daughters but are unable to let them go; these "binding" mothers hold their daughters too closely and may interfere with or even attempt to prevent the development of the daughter's autonomy. Other mothers push their daughters to be on their own too much and are unable to allow for enough intimacy or closeness; the daughters of these mothers often feel "banished," propelled into precocious self-sufficiency and independence. The banishing mother may even insist that the daughter assume the mothering role in the family, and make her responsible for the primary caretaking of her siblings, her father, or even the mother herself.

The binding mother who is unable to let her daughter separate may give either or both of two messages: "you must be like me" or "you must be my extension." In the first instance, the daughter is not expected to develop beyond the parameters of the mother's life. If her mother chose marriage over a career, she should, too. If her relationship to men and collective authority is one of deference and submission, the daughter's should be, too. There is no support to move outside the maternal compound, to have different preferences or to make different decisions. Should the daughter assert her differences, she may be faced with various expressions of disapproval: The mother may threaten to withdraw her love or even to "disown" the daughter, try to make her feel guilty, issue punishments, even feign illness in an effort to command her daughter's conformity to maternal style or image. In response, the daughter may give in to hold her connection with her mother, rebel and break off with her, or inventively lead a "double life."

Melissa was a young woman I first knew in her early years of college. When I met her, she had been living with her boyfriend for nearly two years without her mother's knowledge. She alone answered the phone, and whenever her mother came to visit, her boyfriend stayed with friends. Melissa described her relationship with her mother as always having been close and affectionate but bound round with her mother's high expectations for her only daughter. Unable to challenge her strictly religious mother's image of her as the good, obedient daughter who was "saving herself for marriage" as she herself had done, Melissa even dressed differently when her mother was around, hiding her usual jeans and T-shirts and wearing more "proper" clothes. During Melissa's entire four years at college, her mother never knew that she was sexually active, had left the church, and cared more about parties and friends than the career in nursing for which her mother had groomed her. Finally, the stress of leading her extremely duplicitous life got to be too much for Melissa and she confessed everything to her mother. Mother and daughter went through some stormy confrontations for several months, but the positive bond they had always shared held firm. Melissa's mother disagreed with some of her daughter's choices but came to support her need to define her own life and a new relationship was forged. In this case, a binding mother was able to sacrifice her expectations in order to maintain an ongoing connection with her adult daughter.

A more extreme version of the binding mother appears when the mother merges with the daughter instead of bonding, and expects the daughter to be literally an extension of herself, to live out the unlived portions of the mother's life. The poet Anne Sexton expressed this poignantly in a poem she wrote to one of her daughters:

> I remember we named you Joyce
> so we could call you Joy.
> You came like an awkward guest
> that first time, all wrapped and moist
> and strange at my heavy breast.
> I needed you, I didn't want a boy,
> only a girl, a small milky mouse

> of a girl, already loud in the house
> of herself. We named you Joy.
> I, who was never quite sure
> about being a girl, needed another
> life, another image to remind me.
> And this was my worst guilt; you could not cure
> nor soothe it. I made you to find me.[3]

One woman I know was told directly by her mother that she had been conceived in order to fulfill all the aspirations her mother had had for her own life but felt she had been prevented from realizing. The daughter took them on, sharing especially her mother's interest in classical music and wanting to please her. She became a pianist. The only catch was that whenever the daughter gave a performance, the mother would repeatedly spoil it by telling her she wasn't good enough and sometimes showing her how she, the mother, could do it better. This dynamic is especially common in women's career choices when the initial career of the daughter is in the area that her mother gave up.

A variation of this problem is the common attitude that whatever the daughter does reflects positively or negatively on the mother. A daughter, speaking of her mother in Signe Hammer's book *Daughters and Mothers, Mothers and Daughters*, illustrates this well: "If I was a sterling human being, *she* had done it—it was her achievement. I felt like she was appropriating part of my identity. She would often describe my achievements in terms of her having done it first. She would talk about how bright she had been in high school. She came from a poor farm family and she was very conscious of the fact that she was the smartest person in her high school. I can understand her feeling, but in a way she was telling me that my getting good marks wasn't such an achievement because she had done it first. Even if it was something completely outside her own experience, such as my going to Europe as an exchange student, she would say, 'Oh, this is to be expected from *my* child.' In a way that was all right but there was still a feeling of her not wanting just to participate in my achievements but to diminish them."[4] In this example, the mother merges with her daughter by taking on the latter's achievements as if they were her own.

Other daughters experience their mothers' attempts to merge with them in terms of selective approval and disapproval; the mother approves of anything in the daughter which is like herself and attempts to "disappear" what is not like her through disapproval or dismissal. Betty was a better-than-average student in high school but her real passion was creative writing, at which she was exceptionally talented. Her mother dismissed her writing as "foolishness" and constantly badgered Betty to get higher grades and make the honor roll as she had done when she was in high school. At one point, Betty's mother even got out her old report cards, which she had saved, to show how she had gotten straight *A*s when she was Betty's age. Betty continued her writing, encouraged by several teachers; her mother persisted in ridiculing or ignoring it. But when one of Betty's poems was accepted for publication in a national newspaper, suddenly she was her mother's daughter. Betty's mother bought up a number of newspapers and distributed them to people at her office, describing how *her* daughter had written this poem. Subsequently, she returned to telling Betty that her writing was only a waste of time, she could never make a living at it, and that she should go into business and "get a good job" like the mother's.

Another variant of the attitude that whatever the daughter does reflects on the mother is manifested in women who attempt to control their daughters' unacceptable behavior as if it were their own. An extreme example of this is also presented in Hammer's book, in the following confession from a mother: "I haven't really learned that I am not Helen (her daughter). I am her; she's like another arm, another foot. But now I'm trying to let go of her, to say 'You are a person.' I was never a person to my mother; what I said didn't count . . . If you have another foot or arm, you have control over it. When Helen gets out of control, I feel: my God, that's my foot; what is it doing? I can't let it do that. But I'm beginning to see that I've got to separate myself from her and from my mother too."[5] Such a mother, struggling with a poorly defined sense of herself and not being sure where she leaves off and her daughter begins, repeatedly feels and conveys to her child: "What will people think of *me* if they see your behavior?" The daughter of such a woman may feel she has to withdraw from her mother altogether, simply to feel that her actions and personality belong to her own life instead of being merely an appendage of her mother's.

Not surprisingly, relationships in which the taboo on the daughter's autonomy is the dominant dynamic are often riddled with maternal competitiveness and envy. The mother may consciously want the daughter to succeed in the areas she defines as important, but feel unable to bear it when she does. This is a painful and costly dynamic on both sides. Growing up observing that the culture has traditionally punished women who have actively sought their autonomy and self-interests, the mother pushes down such "selfish" goals and believes the culture's promise that her children will be her personal fulfillment. But individual dreams are very precious; they rarely die, instead go underground. Secretly and often unconsciously, the mother keeps her dreams alive by transferring them to her daughter. Thus the mother can nourish herself in what would appear to be a culturally acceptable way. Yet her daughter's achievements in precisely those areas the mother wanted for herself inevitably elicit envy and rage on the part of the mother. She may grow to hate her daughter because ultimately the daughter has what she herself wanted; the merge doesn't really work. The daughter, meanwhile, is doublebound. If she tries to fulfill her mother, she is baffled and hurt to find that instead of pleasure and approval, there are undercurrents of rage and spoiling. Lacking the support to develop her own life for herself, she may feel stuck forever in a terror of not being able to act independently or of being abandoned if she does.

Some daughters try to avoid getting into this doublebind with their mothers. Diana's mother had been training to be a singer but gave this up when she married. Diana had a beautiful voice and enjoyed singing but her mother made such a fuss over her when she sang that finally she refused to sing altogether. She had really wanted to be a singer herself, she told me, but was never sure whether she would have been being herself or her mother.

Other daughters identify with their mothers' goals for them and don't find out until later that there is a double edge to their mothers' support. Cassie remembers that even in kindergarten, she knew she was going to college; that was all her mother talked about, and early on it was impressed upon her that her parents were "saving for her education." Her father took little interest, but her mother's driving ambition for her oldest daughter was that she should be well educated. Cassie identified with her mother's ambitions for her and, even as a child, dreamed of the kind of career she would have when she grew up. Although her mother took no interest in what kind of work Cassie pictured herself preparing for and often downgraded her daughter's interests and abilities, Cassie always believed that basically she had her mother's support. After completing college, Cassie was determined to go even further in her education and, though struggling financially, got into graduate school and completed her Ph.D. Curiously, she felt, her mother never said anything about her graduate training nor her subsequent career. Once college was finished, her mother never mentioned education again.

At one point, Cassie thought that perhaps her mother didn't realize how grateful her daughter was or how much she had contributed to her daughter's ambition and determination, so she called her mother and told her how much it had meant to her that her mother had always emphasized a college education. To her surprise, her mother went into a two-hour, venomous tirade, beginning with "You always had everything you wanted" and revealing her bitterness that she herself had never gone to college. Once she learned of her mother's feelings, Cassie felt terribly guilty for having had what her mother had not. She recognized that the depth of her mother's envy accounted for the "other side" of her support: downgrading her daughter's interests and abilities, and her total silence and lack of involvement with Cassie's further schooling and career development. Neither mother or daughter ever brought up this subject again, and Cassie continued to feel guilty about her accomplishments, feeling that somehow they had been at her mother's expense. Far from making her mother proud, they had only engendered her anger, an anger that Cassie felt helpless to address and assuage. Cassie was bound to her mother's unfulfilled dream, captured within it, unable either to give it back or claim it wholly for herself. Only with therapy was she able to free herself from being the ongoing carrier of her mother's bitterness and unlived life.

Binding mothers are often women who are insecure about their own lives and choices. If a daughter makes the same choices she did, the mother's sense of self is strengthened and her own choices in life affirmed. If the daughter chooses differently or lives a different life-style from her mother, the mother may be forced to re-examine her own decisions and values. For some women, this will result in a painful awareness of alternatives either not available to them earlier in life or not seriously considered because seen as too risky or culturally unacceptable. The mother who firmly believes that happiness in life is found through marriage and children may feel that something essential to her self is threatened or that she is somehow being personally rejected if her daughter eschews marriage and declares herself happy.[6] If in fact the daughter *is* happy and this is patently obvious, the mother will have to expand her vision of "happiness" to include a choice opposite of her own if she is to maintain both her own values and support her daughter's. But she may also be exposed to a painful questioning of whether she too might have been happy and fulfilled if she had taken a different route. Her daughter's differences may awaken either suppressed or new-found ambivalence in herself regarding her own life. This is especially difficult for the woman who did not make individually thought-through choices to begin with but did what was "expected" of her according to the cultural standards at the time. When a woman's sense of identity is derived not from a personal consideration of what may be right and authentic for her but from "doing the right thing," her daughter's differences may threaten her profoundly. Supporting differences in her daughter requires some sense of inner security and a belief in the right to individual expression that the mother may never have experienced for herself.

The more extreme version of the binding mother, the woman who expects her daughter to live out her unfulfilled dreams, may also be operating out of an identification with traditional cultural images. She may have taken on the belief that children were supposed to be her "life's work," to satisfy and use her skills totally, to be her creativity in life. But children grow up and into themselves and apart from their mothers; at some point, the mother is "out of work." This has been a real dilemma for women who believed that children were supposed to provide the meaning for their lives.

Our culture has traditionally punished women who have actively sought their own self-interest and autonomy, especially if they were mothers. Such women were seen as selfish or even antimaternal. Many women put aside their individual ambitions and dreams in deference to this lack of support, only to revive them in their expectations of their daughters. For many women, the failure of their daughters to carry and fulfill their own unlived lives has been the starting point of a new journey to themselves. If the child does not carry her dreams, the mother may have to face bitter loss, to recognize the lack of opportunities and support in her own life, and to come to grips with where the promises of the culture have been untrue. She may have to come to terms with the limits of her own life and the greater opportunities that may exist for her daughter. But if she can bear the pain and envy that this coming-to-consciousness may bring with it, she may also be able to free herself at last from the cultural dictates and experience a renascence of her own life. New dreams may arise, dreams that can now be embraced by her expanding consciousness and the greater collective opportunities that have emerged from the resurgence of the Women's Movement. Some women discover that support for a more individual life can even come from their daughters. If a mother's own life can be fully supported and lived, she has very little reason to go on binding her daughter's.

Some mothers appear to be the opposite of the binding mother. Instead of holding their daughters too close, they appear to want to keep them as far away and as self-sufficient as possible (that binding and banishing can appear together is evident in the example of Cassie's mother, cited earlier). The banishing mother is often unable to make a bond with her daughter and promotes instead a kind of precocious, brittle independence. The daughter is expected to do as much on her own as possible, often at a very early age. Competence and being the caretaker for others are often stressed at the expense of necessary dependence and closeness. The daughter of such a mother may also be told not to cry, show her feelings, or be needy; she may be shamed for any indication of dependent behavior. Such a daughter may become very independent but not know her own limits or needs, a kind of "superwoman" who takes on responsibilities far beyond her capacity but cannot allow anyone else to help her. She may not know to stop when she is tired, to take care of herself when she is sick, or to make time for her own creativity and pleasure. She may suppress her own dependency needs, as she was taught to do in childhood, or transfer them onto others whom she then can take care of, locating and preserving her own unhealed child only in projection to others.

Kyla was such a daughter. Raised by a mother whose exhausting career absorbed her energy, Kyla's childhood needs were met most often with the instruction, "Cope!" Kyla learned to cope, to care for herself as much as possible, and to stay out of her mother's way. "I learned to cook at the age of three," she said ruefully. "Whenever I cried or didn't know how to do something, I was told to stop being a 'baby.' " As an adult, she was endlessly concerned about her "competence," although she carried the full domestic responsibility for a communal household, which included her husband, their three small children, and four other adults. Frequently she helped her husband with his work as well, yet she described herself as feeling that she never did enough.

When she first came into therapy, she was frequently ill but would carry on until she was on the verge of collapse, then berate herself for being "weak" and "disorganized." She was secretly angry with the others for not doing their fair share, yet, pressed to assert her needs and ask for help, she maintained that their needs were really the legitimate ones since they had "real" jobs and responsibilities outside the home. She never took a day off, had no regular source of child care besides herself, and would become frantic and panicked whenever she was ill. Only by sacrificing her mother's ideal of total "independence" of others, and learning to feel compassion and concern for the overworked child she had been and the overstressed woman she had become, could she begin to balance out the caretaking in her life so that it included care for herself.

The banishing mother is often a woman who received grossly inadequate nurturing herself as a child. She may not know how to nurture her daughter or to facilitate a close bond. In addition, the needs of her own unhealed child may be so great that she will turn even to her daughter for mothering, projecting the possibility of being nurtured and fulfilled herself even to her own child. Or she may be the daughter of an extremely binding mother and be determined to keep her daughter "free" by holding her always at a distance, distrusting closeness. In either instance, the banishing mother's own mother was a poor or distorted role model for her daughter and she may not have had the opportunity for corrective experience. Yet the culture expects her to know how to be a good mother and "do it right," regardless of her own experience with being mothered and the imprint of her personal past.

Another possibility is that the banishing mother, aside from whatever personal problems she may have that make intimacy and closeness with her daughter difficult, may be in unconscious rebellion against the traditional image of woman as "dependent" and "weak." She may want to rescue her daughter from what she sees as women's "fate" by stressing the traditionally male values of toughness, emotional containment, and achievement. The daughter who takes on these values may eschew the female caretaking role altogether or, like Kyla, she may apply these values to it and thus fall into another aspect of the stereotype: woman as "all-fulfiller" of others who has no needs of her own.

Certainly many women today are successful at balancing a close bond with their daughters with support for differences and autonomy. The hard work of the Women's Movement has infiltrated the culture in spite of the backlashes and calls to defensive regression to the "good old days," and has borne fruit. In spite of real difficulties and continued hardships, women and girls have more support today than their mothers did and greater opportunities for a variety of choices. Even the cultural image of "woman" has become more enriched and multifaceted. This has had profound effects on many women who are raising daughters today, enabling them to envision and support a larger arena of self-realization for themselves and their children. It has also enabled some older women with adult daughters to forge new relationships that transform the contrictions of the past and become mutually nourishing to mothers and daughters alike.

In addition, more and more women as individuals are attempting to take responsibility for the imprints of their personal histories and, through psychological and spiritual work, bring healing to themselves and clearer vision to the task of raising their daughters. Such women are not afraid to seek out corrective experience that can address their own unfulfilled needs or training in parenting skills that did not come down to them from their own past experience. Even women with grown daughters are finding this possible; it is never too late to address and change the quality of relationship between mother and daughter, if both women are genuinely willing.

One seventy-year-old woman approached me at the end of a workshop and told me her story. Having felt deeply unloved and rejected herself by her own mother, this woman was determined to "make it different" with her daughter. Through all of her daughter's childhood and adolescence, she lavished care on her, giving her all the things that she had never had. She enjoyed being a mother and believed that her daughter was wonderfully cared for. Thus it was a great shock when, many years later, her daughter, now a middle-aged woman, informed her that she had gone into therapy two years before because of "mother problems." Angrily the daughter revealed how unseen she had felt all through her years of growing up. When her mother protested with reminders of how well she had been cared for, the daughter replied, "You did it for yourself, not for me. You gave me all the things you would have wanted; you never asked if I wanted them, too." Hurt and deeply shaken, the older woman was also astonished and curious. She had believed herself to be deeply in tune with her daughter. How could their perceptions of their relationship be so different? Taking her daughter seriously, instead of just defending her own position, she courageously offered to see her daughter's therapist with her and even go into therapy herself if necessary to explore this and work this out. Her daughter, surprised that her mother would go so far for her and deeply moved, accepted her mother's offer and welcomed her into her therapy. At the time that I met the mother, both she and her daughter were still in therapy. The initial period of airing their discrepant views and exploring the mother's past was painful for both of them, she reported, but each came away with a clearer understanding of the other. The relationship they were now conceiving was a consciously and mutually created one, rooted in the realities and differences of both women instead of conforming to either one's imposed "image."

This is an unusual story, in my experience, grounded in

the courage and essential hunger for truth inherent in both participants. Perhaps as more and more mothers and daughters begin to tell their stories, articulating their own experiences and sorting them out from the images and expectations of each other and the culture at large, more and more authentic relationships will be crafted, allowing for the full humanness of both women. On the human level, truth is never "ideal"; only when ideal images are sacrificed or referred to their transpersonal origins can the truth of human relating emerge.

# 4

# TOUCH IN THE MOTHER–DAUGHTER RELATIONSHIP

Touch is a basic need for all of us at all ages. Babies who are otherwise given perfect physical care but are not cuddled and held literally die. The myth in our culture that women are more at ease with touch than their male counterparts appears, on the surface, to be true. Yet the perfunctory hug or peck on the cheek that many women give each other in greeting may be as bodiless and devoid of emotion as any other superficial gesture that is seen as socially appropriate. Touch that conveys a depth of feeling or seeks a true physical connection may be frightening and foreign to many women despite apparent social ease in this area.

In a culture like ours in which the image of the female body is so profoundly manipulated and women learn early to disown and distort their physical selves, discomfort with touch can hardly be traced to maternal influence alone. Yet many women learn from their mothers what to expect from feminine touch and whether to fear or welcome it. In addition, the mother's relationship to her own body profoundly affects how the daughter views her own. A positive physical connection between mother and daughter can help a woman feel secure enough in her body self to withstand some of the onslaught of cultural pressures to conform to images of the "right" body, while negative experiences with her mother can make her more vulnerable to them.

The session on touch has been the most difficult one in

every course I have taught on the mother–daughter relationship. Even the private journal-writing I ask each woman to do between sessions in response to questions aimed at the topic tends to stop at this point. In the class itself, there are often long, awkward silences during this session. Women have difficulty talking about touch in their experiences with their mothers. While some women have positive memories of maternal touch, others have memories too painful to speak freely about—memories of longing and deprivation or tales of abuse. In addition, because experiences of touch are nonverbal or even preverbal, they may be hard to talk about because they have never been named in words; we may not "know" what our experiences with touch have been until we have struggled to find the words that will make them conscious.

Touch can communicate reassurance, comfort, affection, a sense of the other's "presence," sensuality, sexuality, discipline, limits, rage, hate, and even murderousness.[1] All of these may be experienced with our mothers. Touch carries what I see as the "truth" of the body, a truth not always congruent with what is conveyed verbally and sometimes in stark contradiction to it. Sandy's mother, for example, in the guise of "playing games" with her when Sandy was little, would pinch or slap her daughter until she would cry, then laugh at her because it was "only a game." Since her mother's only other ways of touch were to hit or to groom her, Sandy learned early on that maternal touch was one of the most powerful vehicles of her mother's barely suppressed rage at and resentment of her daughter, a truth that was repeatedly denied verbally by both her mother and her father. Such contradiction is disorienting to a young child, who may eventually have to choose between her own perceptions of what is being communicated nonverbally and what she is being told.

Mothers touch their daughters in various ways. Maternal touch may be affectionate, as in hugging, rocking, holding, and kissing. It may be invasive, as in "inspecting" the child's body for purported flaws or overwhelming her with excessive tickling. Some mothers touch their daughters only to punish them by slapping, pinching, beating them, or jerking the daughter's body around. Finally, some mothers use touch to molest their daughters, arousing them and using them for their own sexual gratification, or touching them in sexual places.[2]

The mother who is able to touch her daughter affectionately and appropriately creates in her a legacy of positive experiences around her body. Feeling that she has been physically as well as emotionally loved, the daughter will carry forth an awareness of her body as positive and as deserving of care and attention. Touching and being touched, instead of being phobically split off or foreign to her, are more likely to be part of her capacity for expressing herself to and receiving from others. The imprint of positive maternal touch creates a kind of "home base" of body experience within the daughter, a base to which she can return for security about herself and to sort out the confusing and distorting messages about her body that may come to her from the culture. The mother's touch carries a "world" within it, a nonverbal world connected with primal experiences of love and security and "home." Even in the daughter's adulthood, her mother's touch may instantly reconstitute that world. One woman discovered this fact in the midst of especially traumatic circumstances. Paula had felt estranged from her mother for some time, an estrangement that appeared to be the natural outgrowth of the difficult times they had had together in her teenage years. A medical emergency when she was in her early twenties became the occasion for the reunion with her mother that created the seedplace for the later close relationship that evolved between them. Paula was rushed to the hospital in great pain, there to discover that she had an ectopic pregnancy and would have to have surgery immediately. By the time her mother arrived, Paula was about to be taken to surgery. Groggy from medication, she was nevertheless fearful of her mother's reactions to her untoward pregnancy. Silently, her mother laid her hand against her daughter's cheek. In that moment, through that touch, a whole history of caring returned to Paula's awareness. The security and love she had known as a child, which had undergirded even her tumultuous adolescence, were conveyed in her mother's presence and she knew that everything would be all right.

For women who have been touched only negatively by their mothers or deprived of touch, the legacy of their childhood experiences is not so benevolent. The woman whose experiences of maternal touch have been predominantly invasive, punitive, or sexual may habitually "armor" her body against touch. This armoring may be expressed in chronic muscle tension or in a psychological sense of the body as "dead" or robotic. In the latter instances, the woman may have a persistent sense of unreality at a bodily level and may fend off bodily sensations both within and without. She may "go dead" when someone else touches her, or repeatedly fail to recognize internal signals of illness or pain. Her repertoire of bodily pleasure may be severely limited or nearly nonexistent; she may live as if she is only in her head. Most likely, she will fail to care adequately for her bodily needs or may replicate her mother's treatment of her in abuse or neglect of her body.

Many women are not "in" their bodies. They may dress attractively and be superficially concerned with physical appearance and well-being but, on a deeper level, see their bodies as "things" to be covered over, decorated, and made pleasing or acceptable to others. Their numbness or hatred toward their bodies may not be discernible to the outside world. One woman I worked with was an exercise instructor. She appeared to be knowledgeable and concerned about physical health and well-being. I assumed she had positive feelings and a positive relationship to her own body as well. Nothing suggested anything to the contrary initially. Then one day, after a particularly painful session, I asked her if she would like a hug. A look of naked longing came into her face for a moment as she said she would. But when I put my arms around her, I was shocked. Her body was limp and lifeless, like a piece of wood. I had the distinct impression that there was "nobody home" on a body–psyche level. Gradually, her true attitude toward her body appeared in both the conscious content of the therapy and in her dreams. In contrast to her knowledgeable concern for others, this woman hated her body and wanted to get rid of it. She overexercised, overdieted, and loathed all bodily manifestations of being female, such as menstruation. Yet the longing I had seen for a moment on her face was also a part of her and it also slowly emerged as a counter to her hatred and an indication of her true need. She was shocked to discover that I didn't share her hatred of being a woman and having female body functions. Though she could rarely let herself, part of her longed to identify with me, to take in a positive valuing of femaleness and a very different picture of the female body than she had ingested from the culture and from her family. Many factors were responsible for this woman's negative attitude toward her body; her experience with her mother was just a small piece. Nonetheless, it was significant, for this woman's mother had withdrawn both touch and other forms of nurturance the minute her younger sibling had been born, asserting, "The baby needs the attention; you're a big girl now." This woman had felt abandoned both physically and psychologically by her mother from that point on.

Some of these symptoms of "going dead" or failing to care for bodily needs may also appear in women who have received little or no maternal touch. In addition, these women may have poorly defined body images and little or no sense of body boundaries. Karen, who had never been touched positively by her mother, confessed to her body therapist that she had no idea how much "room" she took up; she could not conceive of herself as a body in space. She also had no idea of how others perceived her body. Did she seem fat? Thin? Did other people like to touch her or were they repelled? When she finally had the courage to ask for her therapist's feelings during a massage and was told that her therapist liked massaging her, Karen burst into tears. She had never felt loved or affirmed on that level and secretly believed she was repulsive. Ilsa, a woman I worked with in therapy who had never been touched by her mother within her memory, had similar difficulties. She grew up in a bodiless world, surrounded by women—her grandmother, two aunts, and her mother—yet none of the women ever touched each other or her. Ilsa was overweight and felt she needed her weight to have any sense of her body at all; she had no idea, however, of her actual size or physical contours. I proposed that Ilsa lie down on a large piece of brown paper and have a friend trace the outline of her body. She was shocked by the results; in reality, she was much smaller than she thought she was. Like Karen, Ilsa also believed that she was physically repulsive. Both women assumed that this was the reason their mothers never touched them.

Many women who grow up untouched by their mothers feel starved as adults; they long to touch and be touched by their mothers and other women yet are acutely uncomfortable with their own feelings. Their hunger may feel undifferentiated; they may not be able to name it or to imagine that it could ever be expressed and met. They may feel that there is something "wrong" with them for feeling a longing to be touched. They may fear that their fantasies are abnormal or perverse. Our culture, with its strong emphasis on male–female relationships and its tendency to sexualize all touch, offers no help to the woman who is seeking to understand her own needs and find meaning in this area. Without language or models to help her understand her needs to connect with other women, she may pour all of her neediness in this area into relationship with a man, only to feel disappointed, frightened, or angry if he assumes she is issuing a sexual invitation.

The woman who has grown up touch hungry in relationship to her mother may have secret longings to be accepted by another woman, to be held, cuddled, and comforted. She may be intensely curious about women's bodies, long to look at another woman naked without fear or shame. If her own body has been seen as dirty, unacceptable, or loathsome by her mother, she may long to be seen naked herself, to find a renaming and revaluing of herself through the eyes and care of a woman who will accept her body and envision it positively. On a deeper and more primal level, she may yearn to merge into or unite with another body like her own, to dissolve into someone "larger" than herself and magically participate in that person's being and value.

Touch hunger in a woman may coexist with or lead to touch phobia. The untouched woman may vacillate painfully between her longing and her fear. Since touch between women was not modeled in her past as an ordinary, safe, and natural expression of affection and care, it appears as something fearful and outside of her, mysterious, frightening, and unknown. She may express fears of "being a lesbian" if she wants to touch or be held by another woman. Longings to merge may become terrors of dissolving, "being taken over," being "swallowed" by the other. Another common fear in the touch-phobic woman is the fear that she will "want too much," "go too far," that her needs will be insatiable and frighten or repel the other woman. She may fear that if her needs to be touched and held are met, she may "come apart," regress to the level of a little girl. Her adult persona may crumble, she fears, and she may not be able to put it back together again. Part of this fear may be realistic. Being touched does sometimes lower our defenses and allow a more vulnerable self to emerge temporarily. In women for whom touch is not an issue, this experience may be seen as positive and therapeutically sought out. A woman who has had to hold back grief over a substantial loss in her life, for example, may seek the solace of a friend's arms in order to "let go" and be able to express her feeling. Her friend's touch and concern "hold her together," providing a temporary container within which she can safely "come apart." Even quite frightening levels of emotion can be tolerated in the safety of such a container, for the woman knows that, at the end, her ego will reconstitute and her friend will release her back into her normal life, now made easier by the sharing and release of her grief. Most women who are able to seek out and trust such experiences with other women (as well as men) have had similar experiences with their mothers. The mother's physical and emotional presence provided a refuge within which one could come apart temporarily, release one's feelings, and be safely returned to normal life. Repeated experiences like this translate readily into an ability to seek out and trust other women on this level in one's adult life.

For the touch-phobic woman, however, such experience is foreign and unknown. No aspect of it can be taken for granted. She may be afraid of the feelings that come up when she is touched, the tears, rage, wishes, or memories just below the surface. She may resist the undoing of her usual ego boundaries and be terrified at the prospect of letting anyone else—perhaps especially another woman—be her "container." She has not had experience with coming apart and reconstituting. She may truly believe that she might never come together again if she comes undone. And finally, she has no basis for trusting that another woman would help her return to life after such an experience. She may fear instead that the other would take power over her if she dared to trust, mocking or misusing her vulnerability.

Regression may be precisely what's needed for the touch-hungry/touch-phobic daughter. Here, too, her fear of where touch may lead may be realistic, for sometimes touch does take us back to those places in our early experience where we are stuck because of having been wounded or overlooked. In her hungry moments, she may even long to be "reduced to a child" in order to release and be seen in her pain or to get some experience of what she has missed. What her phobic side fails to realize is that the purpose of such regression is to "unstick" those places, to address the needs of the unhealed child and help her to grow into a healthier adult. Temporary regressions in the service of ultimately creating a more grounded, secure adult ego are part of many therapeutic experiences. The careful use of touch is but one of the many vehicles through which this may come about.[3]

Even the most elementary expression of touch may be terrifying to the touch-phobic woman. Jenny's mother was profoundly homophobic. Deeply suspicious of any intimacy between women, she even broke up Jenny's relationship with her best friend when Jenny was eleven years old, years later telling her daughter, "Your father and I were so worried about you." Jenny's mother hated to be touched; whenever her daughter would approach her to hug her or kiss her, she would push her away or try to avoid her. Jenny grew up believing that there was something deeply wrong about affection between women and that all touch was sexual, as her mother apparently believed it to be. Yet secretly, she longed for closeness with a woman that could include touch, and envied her friends who were more at ease in expressing affection than she was. Outgoing and likable, Jenny had many female friends. Affectionate touch would have been a natural component of her caring nature, yet she always felt that something was wrong with her if she wanted to initiate it.

Coming into therapy in her early twenties, Jenny chose to work with an older woman, knowing she had considerable issues with her mother to work through, and wanting to feel better about herself as a "woman." Eagerly she entered into relationship with her therapist, devoured the books she was given on feminine psychology, and felt she was "waking up" to herself as a woman. One thing disturbed her as time went on, however. As she felt closer to her therapist and began to trust her caring, she felt plagued by a recurring fantasy: She wanted to reach out and touch her.

Exploration of this fantasy revealed its simplicity. Even a hug was too much for Jenny to imagine; she simply wanted to touch. Yet every time she felt this, she went into a paroxysm of fear. Something was wrong with her, she felt. She shouldn't want this with a woman. There was something wrong about wanting to touch another woman; touch was to be with a man only. She and her husband touched, she reasoned; why wasn't that enough? Intellectually, she understood some of the effects of her mother's homophobia on her life, but her irrational fears continued.

Two years went by. While the therapy proceeded along well

in other areas, in this one a predictable pattern emerged and was played out again and again. Driven by her longing, Jenny would "confess" her yearning for touch, her therapist would reassure her and encourage her, sometimes even extending her hand, but each time Jenny would fall into terror and pull back. Then her longing would start all over again. Unable either to suppress her longing or to take the risk of expressing it, Jenny felt tortured. Then one day she finally broke the pattern; rising up out of her chair at last, she flung herself at her therapist's feet, wrapping her arms around the older woman's legs and putting her head on her lap. Gently, the therapist laid her hand on Jenny's head and asked, "Do you feel safe now?" There was a long silence. When Jenny finally answered, it was in an altered voice, a voice full of wonder. "Not safe," she replied. "Not safe, but *real.* I feel real. It's not at all like I thought it would be. It's not 'dirty' or wrong. It's like being real for the first time. And you feel real to me, too."

Many women feel unreal in their bodies. For Jenny, this sense was rooted in her mother's distorted ideas about what touch meant between them and her inability to convey to her daughter that her body was also accepted and loved. Some women who have difficulties touching their daughters are as homophobic as Jenny's mother. Some have their own histories of deprivation and abuse to overcome. Some women are torn between husband and daughter, believing that a woman's body is supposed to belong first to her husband and that all touch should go to him. This extremity of patriarchal thinking still exists in our culture. I remember experiencing a vivid version of this in the attitude of a friend when she discovered I was nursing my infant daughter. "Doesn't your husband mind?" she asked. It took me a while to grasp what she was implying, that somehow my breasts existed primarily for his sexual pleasure and that this should have priority over their function in nurturing a child. Since my husband did not share my friend's point of view, I did not feel pressured to choose between my daughter's needs and his pleasure. But many women do feel that they have to choose, not only when their daughters are nursing but at other times in their lives as well.

Sometimes touch is part of the early mother–daughter relationship and then stops. Often this occurs at puberty. The daughter may be told she's "too old" to be cuddled and held, or she herself may withdraw from her mother's embrace. The daughter's developing sexuality and the psychological response it evokes in both women may create an unspoken inhibition against continued touch between them.[4] The Freudian-based expectation that the daughter is to transfer her affection for her mother to her father and then to other men, leaving altogether her primary attachment to a woman, may also play a part here. Often it is the mother herself who socializes her daughter into this expected transfer although it is heavily reinforced in adolescent culture as well.

Mothers who are at ease with their own bodies and relate comfortably to their daughters' bestow a legacy of "being real" as a woman in a female body. They help a daughter to feel real and accepted in *herself*, quite aside from whatever validation and acceptance come to her from a man. Then the latter can be an addition to an already secure sense of self instead of a trigger for the hunger of the unhealed child to come rushing in with her needs to be held and nurtured, to get from a man what she didn't get from her mother. In our culture, it is an accomplishment (and even an individuation task for some) for a woman to feel good about her body "as is" and comfortable with physical intimacy. What she learned from her mother is just one component of how she feels about herself but it is a vital one, addressing or failing to address one of the most basic and human needs we have.

# 5

# MATROPHOBIA AND ITS TRANSFORMATION

### THE ENVELOPE

It is true, Martin Heidegger, as you have written,
*I fear to cease,* even knowing that at the hour
of my death my daughters will absorb me, even
knowing they will carry me about forever
inside them, an arrested fetus, even as I carry
the ghost of my mother under my navel, a nervy
little androgynous person, a miracle
folded in lotus position.

Like those old pear-shaped Russian dolls that open
at the middle to reveal another and another, down
to the peasized irreducible minim,
may we carry our mothers forth in our bellies.
May we, borne onward by our daughters ride
in the Envelope of Almost Infinity,
that chain letter good for the next twenty-five
thousand days of their lives.

—MAXINE KUMIN[1]

Matrophobia, as defined by Adrienne Rich in her book *Of Woman Born,* is the daughter's fear, not of motherhood, but of becoming her mother.[2] Even if the daughter as an adult is on good terms with her mother, she may not want to be like her and may go to great lengths in her own life to ensure that she is not. For some women, this pursuit of "anything but mother" does indeed reach nearly phobic proportions. Yet most of us have moments in which we find ourselves doing things just as our mothers would, possessed by the same attitudes or making the same choices. We yell at a child and hear our mother's words and tone, we give the same advice that we were given at a certain age, we make the same value judgments and then say to ourselves, puzzled and upset, "But this isn't me; it's just like my mother!"

Matrophobia is a fear of being "just like her," a predominant fear among women in our society that sometimes is surrounded with dread and despair. Often women determine that, above all else, they will *not* be like their mothers, and seek to psychically exorcize them from their lives. And yet we are like her. . . .

When I get tense, I can become overly harsh and critical of anyone around me (just like my mother), I can bury myself in work and use it to escape painful emotional situations (just like my mother), I can become cold and remote and try to punish people who hurt me by withdrawing from them (just like my mother). Other women may find themselves being overly submissive to authority—just like their mothers—or falling into their mothers' patterns of being pleasant and agreeable when they are really angry. The list of unwelcome resemblances goes on and on. For some women, being like their mothers is seen as equivalent to being powerless and trapped, having low self-esteem, having a poor relationship with one's body, or being possessed by untamed and abusive power.

On one level, matrophobia is the fear of living out part of the mother's personality or repeating some aspect of her life in one's own. On another level, it is a profound problem with the mother within, an inability to carry her and relate to her. The matrophobic woman attempts to deal with her fears the way any phobic person does: by avoiding as much as possible the conditions that give rise to the fear.

This avoidance may be expressed in several ways. The woman may categorically deny any resemblance to her mother, or seek to undo the resemblance by living as oppositely as possible. She may avoid maternal "territory," or even try to undo the behavior of the mother herself by repeated attempts to change her.

Trying to live oppositely is an especially common response to matrophobia. Such a woman (characterized by Jung as the anything-but-mother daughter)[3] may try to be as opposite from her mother as possible in personality, or may even try to live in exactly opposite ways. The problem is that this extreme an opposition may not truly represent the daughter's own predilections or preferences; she may actually live a "false self" simply to be sure she is not living her mother. The following example illustrates this.

Ann grew up in a house in which neatness and order were extremely emphasized. "There was never a newspaper lying out on a table, never a book out of place on the shelf," she reported. "Everything was perfect all the time. If I wanted to have a girlfriend stay overnight, we had to clean the whole house, including washing the windows! It got so I never asked anyone over because it was such an ordeal." Ann felt constricted and oppressed by her mother's focus on neatness; she continually was criticized for her messy bedroom, and labeled "irresponsible" because of it. She grew up vowing never to be "fanatical" like her mother was. "My college room was wall-to-wall socks," she said.

After she married, Ann deliberately kept what she called a "lived-in" house: Tables and desk tops were piled high with papers, beds were often left unmade, and housework was done irregularly or put off as long as possible. Consciously, Ann felt this as a triumph over her past conditioning, that she could be this "casual," yet she was also frequently uncomfortable with this arrangement. Any unexpected visit from a friend or neighbor brought up painful feelings of guilt and shame, and she even avoided taking her turn at having the neighborhood coffee klatches at her house because she was sure other women would be critical of her housekeeping. When her husband wanted to have some of his business associates over for dinner, Ann would fly into a panic, cleaning all day and feeling exhausted by the time the guests came. Even then, she felt shame throughout the evening, certain that every other woman kept house better than she did. Unconsciously, Ann was still measuring herself by her mother's perfectionist standards, and seeing the casualness she thought she was choosing just as her mother would have seen it: as irresponsible.

By the time Ann brought this issue up in counseling, her discomfort was seriously interfering with some parts of her life. She wanted to start a study group that would meet in her home but was too afraid of "what other people would think" to go through with it. Even her closest friend's reassurance that "nobody cares about this as much as you do" was unconvincing to her. Her internalized mother cared a lot, and was not about to let her off the hook.

After hearing the history of this mother–daughter issue around housekeeping, Ann's therapist asked, "What would it be like if you kept house *for* yourself instead of *against* your mother? What would you do differently?" Ann was shocked by the question. She hadn't really thought about keeping house to please herself; she just didn't want to be like her mother. With more reflection, Ann realized that she was replaying the whole relationship of exacting mother and rebellious daughter inside of herself. Her mother's perfectionism no longer came from the outer voice of her actual mother but was embedded in Ann's own guilty conscience and projected to others as imagined critics, while the rebellious daughter within her was defiantly messy to counteract the impossible standards to which Ann still secretly gave authority. Ann was perpetually doublebound in this place, loyal to both sides, but never able to get herself out of the dilemma. Her conflict kept both her mother's standards and a reactive child self alive and continually at odds with each other.

Her therapist's question had jolted Ann out of the old framework. As she began to consider what keeping house for herself would be like, she realized that, quite aside from what her mother would think, being very messy made *her* unhappy.

She learned that she preferred a somewhat neater house. Her mother's standards were too extreme for her, but so was the stance of the reactive child. Neither represented what truly fit her as an adult. Once she had discovered her individual preferences as an adult, she was able to relate to her inner mother differently, no longer playing out the rebellious or guilty daughter but asserting her independently conceived standards.

Some women like Ann learn to assert their own values within an area that had previously been dominated only by their mothers; other women attempt to deal with matrophobia by trying to avoid the mother's "territory" altogether.[4]

This pattern was redoubled in the case of Amy, whose mother Jane was also living out a matrophobic response pattern. Jane had grown up as the only, neglected daughter of a woman who had conceived her out of wedlock and who saw her child as a serious interference with her acting career. Jane was shuttled from relative to relative while her mother pursued her career; she rarely even saw her mother. Vowing never to neglect her children the way that she herself had been neglected, Jane became her mother's opposite. Immediately upon marrying, she gave up a promising career as a dancer and settled down to devote herself to her husband and the seven children who came along in rapid succession. Amy was the middle of those children. She remembers her mother as "Mom with a capital M," a passive, negative martyr who sacrificed herself for her family. Her mother's motto was "I live to serve" but, in fact, she demanded that all of her children serve her. Terrified that she would become just like her mother, Amy threw herself into the pursuit of a career as an artist. Babies and domestic life were a "trap," she felt, a way of life she wanted no part of. Amy was conscious of the identification that lay beneath her antimaternal stance; she feared that if she ever did have children, she would be "doomed" like her mother, forever split off from her creativity and bound to devour everyone around her.

Matrophobia and the attempts to resolve it by denying any

resemblance to the outer mother or by trying to get rid of the inner mother are steeped in magical thinking on the part of the daughter. The daughter unconsciously believes that if any part of her is like her mother, it will somehow reconstitute the whole; she will lose her own identity and become her mother. Identification with the child's perspective and undeveloped ego is central in this dynamic; the daughter thinks, "If I am at all like my mother, other people will see me the way *I* saw her and react to me the same way I reacted to her." In these matrophobic moments, the daughter does not grasp the strength of her own personality nor the relativity of her mother's power; she is reacting as if she is still in the child position, and mother is all.

What is striking in this phenomenon is the depth of the fear and the entrenched belief in the mother's negative power—so much so that if the daughter is anything like the mother, that power will reconstellate and have the same effects on others as it had on the daughter, or so the daughter believes. This fear makes sense from the limited perspective of the child, but matrophobia is a phenomenon in adult psychology. Moreover, it is strikingly prevalent among women in our culture. I have never given a lecture or done a workshop or class on the mother–daughter relationship and spoken about the anything-but-mother daughter without seeing nearly every head nodding in recognition and agreement.

The truth is, we *are* like our mothers at some level, and there is no getting away from this. Each of us carries at least some of her mother within her; each of us has introjected her to at least some extent. This inner mother may function as a "voice," a pattern of reaction, a certain set of opinions directed at ourselves or at others. We may fall into feeling manipulative or powerless or critical just like her. But it is very important at this point to differentiate between the outer mother and the inner. The outer mother may change or die, while the inner mother goes on in a fixed pattern. While the outer mother may have gone beyond the woman she was then, through her own development or because of different circumstances, the inner mother may remain the mother we experienced at five or fifteen. On the other hand, the outer mother may be utterly entrenched, more fixed than ever in her patterns, and then we despair about the parts of us that are like her; but it is important to differentiate between outer and inner mothers even if they appear to be alike. With the inner mother, we may have more opportunities for transformation.

The inner mother may begin to function as what Jung calls a shadow figure in us, an involuntary pattern of behavior that is not acceptable to our egos and that we struggle to suppress or readily project onto others. She may come up unconsciously as part of our own behavior, and be easily visible to others but not to ourselves. But the shadow, as Jung speaks of it, is not necessarily bad or fixed; it can also embody something that hasn't fully developed, that has been kept back because we see it so negatively. There may be great value in the shadow and also a possibility for its transformation and growth. The inner mother may be able to develop and may even *want* to develop in ways the outer mother cannot. We will come back to this.

We are also *not* our mothers; the introjected mother is embedded in a different context because she's inside of *us*. The inner mother is part of a *different* whole, a different personality complex; thus, we can never be "just like our mothers." Because of this, our inner mothers may have different effects on those around us than our outer mothers had on us.

This is something I first learned from my daughter, when I became aware of how different her responses were from those of the unhealed child within me. When I was a child, my mother expected me to learn how to do things instantly and perfectly; if I didn't catch on quickly and didn't do it right the first time, she would fly into a fit of rage and leave the room. As an adult, I have at times a tendency toward this same pattern of impatience; its existence is extremely painful to me and I have tried to protect my daughter from it, mostly by trying to connect her with other people who can teach her well or by trying fiercely to discipline this reactivity in myself so it won't land on her. It has taken me years, even for myself, to learn how to carry a whole learning process, to tolerate having difficulty at the beginning while a skill is new and to stay with the process long enough to get more and more proficient. I have difficulty not abandoning myself in a learning process, just as my mother abandoned me.

When my daughter was little, I would manage not to fly into my mother's rage when she was learning something new, but often I could not see her through the whole process. I would show her how to ride a bike, for example, and then leave her with it; I could not help her over and over. I felt terrible about this and inadequate as a mother because I wanted to help her more, but I couldn't stay with it without becoming horribly impatient—just like my mother. Then suddenly I began to watch my daughter and to notice how she reacted to this. Unlike me, she was very persistent and stayed with the task until she learned it. Because the rest of me was genuinely caring about her and we had a basically positive bond, her desire to please me led her to take on my expectations of fast learning, but in her this transmuted into a huge desire for mastery and she would stay with the task until she accomplished it. Now, in her teens, she is generally very quick to learn, has an enormous capacity to persist in learning, and is teaching *me* how to tolerate mistakes or having to do things more than once. By teaching me more tolerance and modeling a different style of learning, my daughter participates in healing the effects of my mother on me. Partly, she is able to do this because she had a different mother herself. At one level, my daughter has become a role model for a part of me that is younger than she is and still struggling to grow past my mother. Thus does the pattern come full circle, in quite a different way than my matrophobic side alone would have imagined it. By responding differently to my mother in me out of her own experience of being mothered, my daughter changes the effects of my mother on me and teaches a different way to my unhealed child.

On one level, the introjected mother is a learned pattern; we have this in us because it is what was modeled for us. We tend to respond in the same ways that were modeled for us in areas in which we have not yet developed our *own* selves, as in the case of Ann and her housekeeping. Therapy for this level consists of *relearning,* of taking on the maternal introject and re-educating it in ourselves. Thus women who have been abused by their mothers, for example, can learn, with help and remothering from a nonabusive person, how to deal with frustrations and difficulties without abusing either their children or themselves.

On another level, the introjected mother is our own psychological dynamic that may carry its own urge toward transformation. In a sense, it pushes our mothers forward into new development, not outwardly by changing the actual mother but inwardly by re-educating ourselves and thus having a new base from which to stand against the maternal pattern. For example, Ann can say no to her perfectionist impulses by recalling her *own* standards and values and asserting them against the "shoulds." Most of us would like to change our actual mothers; we may only be able to change the mother within us. Many of us would like to rescue our actual mothers; we may be able to rescue only the internal versions. But, unlike the outer mothers, the internal versions may *want* to be rescued. The inner mother may function like an unconscious legacy, needing and wanting to be made conscious and helped, whereas our outer mothers may not want this at all or be capable of it. But consciousness requires of us a responsibility as well; there is a burden involved in becoming conscious. We must be willing to *suffer* our mothers within us, to see to the roots of their behavior within us, and to forgive and transform it in ourselves. We may also be able to see through to our common lot as women, finding in our inner mothers responses to powerlessness, perversions of spirit, or distorted potentials. Becoming conscious of the negative effects of our mothers on our lives is not enough; it is as if we must take our

mothers *in* and carry them psychologically as they once carried us physically.

It is not enough to free ourselves individually or even to seek out better models and healthier experiences; we must also come to terms with our personal legacies and find what they require of us. We must get to know the inner mother, to turn attention to her and discover what her presence in us means and how she might be of value to us. By pondering her presence and manifestations, we can seek to understand this part of ourselves and raise the following kinds of questions (this kind of work might be done in meditation or a journal): Who is this inner mother? What is she like? Why does she come up destructively, if she does? What development of our own do we need, to teach her a different way of responding? How does she feel about us, see our projects, our children? What qualities does she carry that might be useful or balancing to us if they could begin to function in a nondestructive way? Perhaps she is more ordered than we are but embodies order in an unrelated, military rigidity. Perhaps she is more outgoing but seeks to dominate and overrun the other. Perhaps she is envious of others who have what she wants but uses her envy to attack and spoil rather than let it tell her what she really wants. Perhaps she carries a legitimate need for attention but has to express it through manipulation or getting sick. If we can see through to the core of the inner mother's qualities, over time and with effort we may be able to abstract her qualities objectively from their negative hull and to use them productively for our own lives.

By turning toward our inner mothers instead of trying to rid ourselves of their unwanted tenancy within us, it is as if we put our mothers into a different context, into the wholeness of ourselves. In this way, we become their matrix; in a sense, we become pregnant with our mothers and carry the possibility of their transformation and rebirth within ourselves.

I once had a moving and instructive experience of the beginning of such a process of rebirth in a therapy session of my own. In one session I became just like a part of my mother: cold, remote, shutting out my therapist completely just at a particularly tender moment. Usually my therapist responded with aplomb to my shifts and tolerated them, but this time she was hurt and angry. She told me at the end of this session that she really didn't like this part of me, didn't like my mother within me. Usually I've despaired over this sudden coldness in myself because I know it hurts people and I have often felt trapped inside of it when it comes up. Ordinarily, I would have felt badly about its appearance, but this time I was hurt in return. I wanted my therapist to like all of me, even my cold inner mother. This seemed quite unreasonable, even to me; I thought it was just the child in me wanting everything to be loved, but I was still surprised by my feeling. Pondering this for a time, I wondered what it was from this side of myself that wanted to be liked, and why, when it was so destructive. Suddenly I had a clear picture of my mother within me; I could feel her, this cold and remote woman whose real-life model had such difficulty with intimacy. But unlike my outer mother, who resists self-awareness and has never acknowledged any sense of responsibility or guilt for her actions, this woman was aware of her limits and felt them keenly. She couldn't change—she knew she was cold and remote and harsh—but, in my therapist and me, she saw a difference, something outside of her, an ability to relate warmly, that she had no access to herself. In my image, she was drawn to my therapist especially. It seemed that she just wanted to sit next to her, to be near someone who was really different from herself, to make contact with a different way of being even if she herself couldn't be that way. Within this image, I could feel her sadness (and sadness for my real mother as well) and the wish for change even in something so entrenched and stuck within her armor. I began to realize that maybe gradually my inner mother could learn a little and draw something from the woman who was so very unlike her and so very important to me.

One woman in one of my mother–daughter classes reported experiencing her alcoholic mother as a "killing force," but had the sense that if she could dance that, become that force, she might learn about it and not be so fearful of it in herself. Another woman imaged her mother's transformation in a song that she wrote. This woman's mother was a particularly self-effacing woman who always put the man first; her daughter had always felt a great longing for more connection with her mother, and struggled with her own sense of self-effacement. What was particularly painful to her was that her mother was dead; all possibility for reconnection seemed lost until she conceived the transformation depicted in this song:

> Mother, Mother, your pain was my milk,
> sap of my branching bones.
> They are strong now, like cold steel,
> but have always cried for sun.
> My birth ripped you only once—
> you have been spared the others;
> but I, watching myself emerge,
> don't know whose blood this is.
> Mother, Mother, your tears flow
> in my salted body
> and tides pull my life over yours.
> Our speech becomes clearer as I wake
> and your death grows rich in ease.
> Mother, Mother, welcome into my form;
> let us breathe together.[5]

In this poem, the daughter's transformation enables her to revision what was previously only a legacy of pain. Through her own waking, her dead mother is revived and restored, welcomed into new form within her daughter. Mother and daughter breathe new life together. This is especially dramatic in its musical form, for the song was written in an entirely minor key which changes to a major key with the words "welcome into my form."

Instead of trying to cut our mothers out of ourselves, we need to welcome them into our forms, to relate to them anew, and let our fullness and the consciousness we struggle for transform them as once they transformed us. But to bring this about, we need to look more deeply at the unhealed child.

# 6

# THE UNHEALED CHILD: PARTIAL SOLUTIONS AND HEALING POSSIBILITIES

When I was a child, I had a recurring fantasy that was so powerful, it was almost hallucinatory. I would imagine that I heard someone crying, and this crying was so poignant, so compelling, that I would start to leap up from my bed each time to try to find that person and take care of her. I had no idea until much later in life that the crying was part of myself and that it was myself I'd have to tend. Instead, I found that crying over and over in other people by becoming a "caretaker." Tending that crying child in others is just one instance of what some of us have done with the unhealed daughter within us, what Adrienne Rich has called that "wildly unmothered"[1] place in us all.

The unhealed daughter is full of yearnings, rage, hurt, and legitimate needs which were not met in her experiences with her mother. She is a "child place" within us that continues to be present and felt or denied within our adult lives.

The unhealed child has yearnings: yearnings to be nurtured, supported, cared for, to be "special," the "apple of someone's eye," yearnings to be held, cradled—not just literally but to have one's life cradled—to be held *enough*. The unhealed child longs to have someone care only about her, put her first and at the center, not to stay there forever but so she can grow from a base. When this is possible, she can then help us learn to put ourselves first in our lives, to make a center out of our own beings instead of displacing the center onto someone else, as we women have traditionally been taught to do.

The unhealed child wants what she never had. She may stay stuck forever in loneliness, covering over her needs; in rage that insists on being heard; in the need to be seen by her mother; or in her list of grievances. Or she may be denied altogether by the adult woman who takes on a brittle "that was then, this is now" attitude that puts aside both the pain and the needs of this inner place. More often, though sometimes secretly, she hangs on forever to the past, does not let go of her mother or of her expectations/demands that the mother be there for her. She may go on forever being a daughter, trying to win her mother's approval, trying to get love, attention, and final acceptance from her.

This can be an enormous demand on the mother: an adult daughter who will not let go, will not accept what was, will not accept the mother's limits or the limits of her childhood experience. But this is also torturous for the daughter, who may repeatedly experience the same responses from her mother and react as if she is somehow neurotically "stupid," not learning from rejection or coldness or lack of fulfillment but repeatedly trying to get something different. If our friends treat us badly or are not supportive time after time, most of us move away from them. Yet we hang onto our mothers.

The unhealed child hangs on in need, rage, and indignation; she insists that her mother can and should fulfill her "role," be a "real" mother. The image of what mother "should" be is insisted on, even if her mother has never been like that image and has little interest or capacity for it. This insistence may be present throughout the adult daughter's life.

Marcy was a gift giver; for years she had been trying to give her mother the perfect gift, the gift that would not only please her mother but would "get through" to her and enable a common bond, that would finally dissolve the barrier that had always been between them. In spite of the fact that her mother was continually puzzled by Marcy's gifts and responded with either bewilderment or indifference, Marcy was sure that if she just kept trying, sooner or later she would pull her mother toward her.

One year she bought her mother a book of Käthe Kollwitz's etchings. She was vaguely aware that many of these etchings depicted mothers with dead children and wondered, just before she sent it off to her mother, if this carried some sort of secret message. Consciously, however, she just wanted to "share" something with her mother that had moved her deeply. Her mother, a prim and proper, emotionally distant woman who disdained displays of feeling, was baffled by the gift which she found distasteful. The most polite response she could manage was, "Well, they certainly aren't pretty." Another year, feeling deeply for what she saw as her mother's deprived and unsensuous life, Marcy bought her mother the most exquisitely beautiful piece of lingerie that she could find. Again her mother was baffled and put off by what she considered too intimate a gift from her daughter; moreover, the petticoat was unlike anything she had ever worn and, as she informed her daughter, "I'm too old to start wearing this kind of thing now." The next year, Marcy tried a different tack. Thinking back over her mother's career as a businesswoman and seeing her as courageously standing against the criticism she had received for being a working mother in the 1950s, Marcy decided that what she and her mother had in common was feminism. So she sent her mother a year's subscription to *Ms.* and tried to engage her in discussion of various articles. Finally, Marcy's mother told her outright that she really preferred other kinds of women's magazines and could not identify with "women's libbers."

In spite of consistently negative responses, which were congruent not only with her mother's personality and preferences but also with the distance she had always maintained with her daughter, Marcy continued her search for "just the right gift." Each gift contained the unspoken and partly unconscious message: "Come close to me; see me; let me be close to you." Underlying that was a tenacious demand: "Be the mother I need you to be, not the mother you are." Unable to bear the pain of the vast differences between herself and her mother or of her mother's strong preferences for separateness instead of intimacy, Marcy persisted in trying to make her mother over into the closely involved and supportive presence she felt she had missed. She needed this presence to bolster and nourish her own adult life.

Deborah's adult relationship with her mother followed a similar pattern. Deborah's great dream in her early twenties was to "make it in the big city" as an actress. Soon after graduating from college, she determined to leave her small hometown in Ohio and move to New York City. Her mother, who was disappointed that her daughter showed little interest in marrying and raising a family, strongly disapproved of this move and expressed great doubt about her daughter's career and her ability to live independently.

The transition to New York was difficult for Deborah, and the competition in her field much more intense than she was prepared for. Often discouraged and depressed, Deborah repeatedly turned to her mother, pouring out her despair and disappointments. Each time, she hoped her mother would encourage her, would lift her spirits and express a positive belief in her daughter's dreams. But, each time, her mother only commiserated and told her to come home. "Your old bedroom is still available" was her standard response when her daughter was feeling low. Despite her mother's overt disapproval of her move East and her insistence that having a family was "enough of a career for a woman," Deborah turned to her again and again, each time expecting support and encouragement, each time disappointed and hurt when they were not forthcoming. Still she persisted, endlessly hoping to call forth a different kind of mother.

The "finally she'll see me" fantasy is based on the entrenched belief in the unhealed child that both the desire to see the daughter as she is, and the capacity to do so, are actually present in the mother and that she is as centered on her daughter's life as the daughter herself is. Yet Marcy's mother was preoccupied with the further development of her own life now that her children were grown. Relieved to be finished with the everyday demands of a family, she genuinely did not want a closer involvement with her daughter. Deborah's mother was focused on defending the position that she had taken when Deborah left home, and insisting that her values were the only viable ones; each despairing of her daughter only served to bolster her beliefs. Both mothers were, in a sense, totally true to themselves and their own values, but this did not address the unhealed child in either of their daughters.

We need mothers, even as adults, to be strong, whole women who like themselves and are fed enough themselves to nourish us. We need them as models and contributors to our own fullness as women, as visions of what a woman can be. We may find part of this experience in relationship to other women in our lives: aunts, grandmothers, friends of our mothers, stepmothers, teachers. But the unhealed child is still impatient, still crying; she wants her *own* mother, an origin that is a whole . . . and like a child, she wants to push out anything noxious about this origin, push out the recognition that limitedness and pain and rejection and despair are part of wholeness, too. The child level cannot make meaning out of negative experience; it rails against it, acts out, pushes back, tries to punish or protest it. It takes the fuller adult to raise the questions of meanings about experience as it *is*, not just as it approximates the ideal.

The bond we insist on with our mothers is culturally induced; we may be more flexible in our expectations of grandmothers, aunts, friends. But our mothers carry the archetype, as well, and we do need connection with that. We have not been allowed to see or value where and how that greater Mother comes through, nor been taught how to relate to Her. And, more deeply, there is the sense of "belonging" to that actual mother and a demand/question formed around that;

she gave me birth; I *came* from her; how could she not love me or be more limited than I *need*?

We hang on because there's a numinosity in this, a "charge" attached to mothers, unlike the charge attached to any other relationship in our lives. Mother/origin/cradle/source: something greater that we came from and belong to. An old chant speaks the image we long to be able to find in our mothers: "Love is the only law I know/by naught but love may I be known/and all that liveth is my own/from me they come, to me they go." The speaker in this chant is the Great Goddess imaged as the origin and end of all life; we've hungered for this sense of belonging with our mothers.

Adult women relate to the unhealed child within themselves in various ways. They may project her to others and take on the mother or caretaker role themselves, either mothering actual children ("doing for them what was never done for me" is how many women describe it) or finding the child part of other people. They may become exquisitely sensitive to the lonely little boy in a husband or lover, even seek that out in a man, transferring their own neediness to him and nourishing it there. If he then plays out the little boy, the woman may feel vaguely hurt and used, unconsciously experiencing the transfer of her inner child to him as some kind of robbery of herself. The woman who relates to her unhealed child by having children herself may genuinely enjoy mothering and get vicarious fulfillment through meeting her children's needs, but a problem may arise as her children become more and more independent of her. To keep her own inner little girl alive, she may "need to be needed" by her children, and infantilize them in order to stay connected with this unknown part of herself. Part of the loss that many mothers experience as their daughters grow up is the loss of what seemed like a second chance at girlhood, a more nourished girlhood than they themselves experienced. Still other women take their unhealed child selves into work in the helping professions; taking care of others becomes a career. This kind of work may bring enormous satisfaction but, if they are not

simultaneously caring for themselves and instead insist on locating the unhealed child "out there" in the needy other, it may be very difficult for them to allow their patients or clients to grow beyond a child's level of need.

Women also try to take care of their unhealed inner daughters by trying to find a mother in a man. They may believe the traditional message that they will be "taken care of" if they get married, or they may marry a man who is much like their real mothers.[2] The latter situation is usually unconsciously sought out, yet may afford the woman a fine opportunity to address her dynamics with her mother in another arena if she can become conscious of the similarities between her mother and her husband and work toward her own growth beyond the old patterns. Since it is more acceptable for an adult woman to be dependent on a man than to depend on her mother, some women will turn to men to fulfill their unmet child needs. Much of the neurotic attachment and dependency that women get into with men is rooted in the needs of the unhealed child.

Still another way that women relate to their unhealed child selves is to deny them altogether. These women, often forced to grow up at too young an age and to assume adult responsibilities early on in life, are often highly competent caretakers who deny vehemently any neediness in themselves. Dependence and whatever is seen as "regression" are particularly taboo behaviors for these women.

There are many positive ways to approach the unhealed child in ourselves. First, we can learn to identify her needs and claim them as legitimate: needs for attention, affection, praise, unconditional love, play. We can bring these needs to the surface and refuse to label them "bad." One of the reasons that we suppress these needs as adults is that they often bring painful childhood memories with them, memories of how we were punished or distorted or our needs unmet as children. We need to allow these memories to come up and be felt, for they belong to our wholeness; we need to mourn with the child, grieving over her deprivations, pain, and unfulfilled longings. Sharing childhood pain with a friend or therapist can lead to an emotional companioning that assuages the grief of the unhealed child; she no longer feels totally alone, totally unseen in her hurts. (Thus, one woman I worked with in therapy who had been severely abused as a child told me that the worst of it was not the abuse itself but that there was no one to comfort her afterwards, to be with her in her fear and her pain.) Emotionally companioning the child within by being willing to listen to her complaints and hurts can eventually lead to new growth and a fresh flow out of her stuckness.

Perhaps the most difficult piece of grief work inherent in coming to terms with the unhealed child is the adult recognition that something really has been lost, that the child's level of need can never be met in its original context. We will not ever have that good childhood that might have optimally nourished our true selves. This does not mean that the childhood experience cannot be addressed or healed, only that new channels have to be found to meet this part of ourselves. Deeper questions of meaning come up when the woman is truly able to accept that her childhood experience was as it was and that her mother can no longer make it better. She can then turn to the questions: What did it mean for my life that I had this mother? Who or what did I have to become because of this experience? What have I developed in myself that might not have developed had my experience been different? Many women find strengths in themselves they may not have seen before.

Raising questions of meaning and re-evaluating ourselves are not enough; we must also begin to care for the child within, actively to make room for this part of ourselves in our adult lives. What are her needs? Does she need time to play? to create? Does she need places to "show off" her skills or enthusiasms? What kind of stimulation does she need (colors, music, playthings)? Can we mother our inner children the way we might mother an outer child or support a lover or husband, by giving interest and time to ourselves, providing sustenance and enrichment?

If the inner child is being cared for in other ways, some women are able to reassess their mothers from a more adult perspective and seek out a new kind of bond. They may be able to ask: Is there anything she can give me in the present? Can I give up my role of child with her? If so, on what basis can we now meet each other and relate? Are there interests we share as adults? Can I see her life in context and accept her limits? Can I let go of the demand that she be the one to care for me in a deep way just because she's my mother? For some women, finding the answers to these questions may lead to a new, limited relationship with their mothers—or it may lead to letting go altogether, letting pretense or false bond die and accepting that there will be no other relationship.

Evelyn's mother was continually critical and cruel. If Evelyn shared her joys, her mother would counter with envy, "You always had it easy." If she shared her painful moments or despairs, her mother would add to her hurt with criticism. For much of her adult life, Evelyn tried to find some way to connect with her mother, to make some kind of positive bond, but was always attacked for her efforts. If she tried to confront her mother's hurtful behavior, she was met with rage and virulent put-downs. But, for a long time, Evelyn could not give her mother up. She believed that if she just tried hard enough, she would find the key that would unlock her mother's love and enable the relationship to begin in a more positive way. Only when she began to put more focus on relating to her inner child and began to take care of her own needs, and when she developed a friendship with an older, nurturing woman who provided a contrast to her mother, did Evelyn realize that she was never going to get anything she needed from her mother. She realized that she was the dumping ground for her mother's rage. That was the only bond between them. With great effort, she let go, refused to provide opportunities for her mother to criticize her, and withdrew from the relationship. Secretly, her child self hoped that this would get through to the mother and that her mother would come after her, but this did not happen. Instead, her mother was indifferent to Evelyn's withdrawal and made no move to counter it or reconnect. At first Evelyn felt extremely guilty, as if she had broken some deep taboo. "She's my *mother*," Evelyn said. "How can I turn my back on her?" Slowly she realized that her mother was also responsible for maintaining the relationship and was making no move to do so, that, in fact, it was Evelyn who had held the relationship together all through the years and who had always taken the initiative.

Evelyn has learned to live without a relationship to her mother; at times, it still hurts her child self deeply; and, at times, she still feels guilty. But she has also learned to search our nurturance in other places, to spread out her need for mothering, opening toward others who are more able to care than her mother was. Of special importance to her is her relationship with her older friend Alice who has been consistently supportive and interested in Evelyn's life. "Sometimes I wish I'd been born to Alice; I watch her with her kids and realize what it would have been like. But then I realize that we would have had our problems, too, ordinary ones, I guess, but no mother and daughter relationship is perfect. But I'm really glad that I met her at this point in my life, instead, because now she is more than a mother to me; she is also my friend. We share interests that we might never have gotten to as mother and daughter."

Spreading out the need for mothering can include seeking out mutually supportive relationships with other women, identifying with the Women's Movement, with women in history or literature or art. It means actively participating in the mothering of the unhealed child by connecting her with the resources she needs in the present. Spreading out the mothering may also lead to a reassessment of people in the past, a consideration of other women one might have drawn deeply from at one time or another. In Evelyn's case there was a camp counselor, Marie, who had given Evelyn a great deal of encouragement and praise for her athletic prowess in her teens. Reassessing this woman's influence, she realized that in Marie's eyes she was strong and competent, of value as a person. Although Evelyn never saw Marie after her teens, she was able now as an adult to think back to Marie's presence in her life and to bring her view to bear upon the distortions of self-image engendered in her relationship with her mother. Ultimately, she was able to relativize her mother's view of her, realizing it was the distorted image of a woman who was unable to love her instead of the truth of her character. Gradually, Evelyn has come to identify more substantially with the way she has been seen by people who have loved her, both in the past and in the present.

Taking the unhealed child's needs seriously, but letting go of our daughterhood; suffering the pain of what we didn't get, without becoming masochistic; and letting go of the wish/demand that our mothers mother us are not easy. It means accepting our past as it was, while carrying the legitimacy of our needs. It means accepting the limits of what we experienced with our actual mothers, and bearing the pain of realizing that the childhood experience with her is over. In a sense, it means letting go of the claims of the "daughter" role and allowing our mothers to let go of the role of "mother" as well. Something is lost when the child's needs have not been met in childhood but there may also be a richness gained. Deprivation can sometimes stimulate development of independence, strength, and a capacity for suffering and transformation that, when balanced by being nurtured as an adult, can lend depth and breadth to the adult personality.

The longings of the unhealed child can also be transmuted into a powerful social concern. Adrienne Rich suggests that the passion of the unhealed child—carried by the adult woman—can become a political passion to create a different kind of world, one in which women are more valued, where bonds between women are more emphasized and held as vital to mothers and daughters alike, and in which oppressive institutions and cultural demands that all women fit certain roles and expectations are continually challenged.[3] Thus the unhealed child may engender enormous creativity. The experiences of false roles and false connections can generate a rage and passion that seek to create something new—not by endlessly trying to change our mothers, but to change the world. On a more personal level, this is what many of us seek to do with our daughters, to forge new visions of support and bonding, and create something different from our own personal histories.

Finally, a spiritual dimension can be recognized in the longings of the unhealed child. Where did I come from? To whom or what do I belong? What is my matrix? What can sustain and nourish my life? How am I to understand the pain and suffering and deprivation I've experienced? These are not only secular questions about our human relationships but spiritual questions as well.

The birth giver of our lives, in this context, becomes tied up with the questions of destiny and meaning. "Mother" in this context becomes huge, a power not only beyond us but beyond the human realm. And all that we've connected with our human mothers and our common experiences as women, mother and daughter alike, all those places of bondings or missed bondings were once sacred images: pregnancy and birth, menstruation and menstrual blood, female bodies, female sexuality, the life cycle of girl–adult–old woman were all divine images. Nurturance, cradling, and sustaining life as well as banishing, rejecting, and depriving were not only connected with experiences of human mothering but experienced in relationship to the Divine as well.

Set in a spiritual context, Mother becomes larger, her birth giving seen not only as literal, as we experience our human birthings, but also as a paradigm of the creativity of the universe, of creativity itself. Her womb is no longer only the literal space that sheltered a human being, but also an image of that which gestated all of life, upon which life is dependent.

Set in this context, the longings of the unhealed child—to have an origin that she is connected to, to be held, nourished, cared for, sustained, to see Her body and come to know and value her own, to have a model of feminine strength and wholeness and carry it into her own life, to have an ongoing connection she can depend on that gives a kind of backbone of feminine meaning to her life—all these longings become revisioned. And even being a daughter takes on a spiritual meaning and becomes a spiritual quest. So, too, the suffering—the sense of being abandoned and not having enough resources of one's own, the terror of being devoured by a power greater than oneself, the painful estrangements, the rage on one's own behalf and list of hurts, the development of strength and independence and individuality vis-à-vis these experiences—these too become part of a much larger drama.

Part of the reason it's been so hard for us to let go of our mothers, and part of the reason our longings and demands can get so ferocious and not let either our mothers or ourselves go, is that there is a larger picture behind this whole relationship, a picture that belongs to us and that we need but that has been blotted out by centuries of suppression. It is not a human picture but that is precisely why it is so compelling; it bears the mark of the archetype, a compelling power we both long to connect with and fear. We are infinitely tied up with *this* meaning of Mother and Daughter, but it's been lost to our culture almost completely, loaded onto one often very limited human being who can't carry it and who needs its presence for her own sense of sustenance and meaning as much as we do. Pieces of the archetype come through her mothering but she is not that great a Mother, cannot carry it all—and yet we need an experience of that great a wholeness to envision and move towards our own.

# 7

# LIFESOURCE: INTRODUCTION TO THE GREAT MOTHER

> "In the start of time, splendor appeared," Merope was chanting. "It was the Mother. She was all that was. She divided the sky from the sea and danced upon the waves. A wind gathered behind Her from Her swift dancing. When She rubbed this wind between Her hands, it became the Great Serpent. She took him to Her and loved him, and a great egg grew within Her and She became a Dove. The Dove-Mother brooded over the egg until it was ready. Then out of the egg came all things—sun, moon, stars, earth, mountains, rivers, and all living creatures. The splendor of the Mother flowed through everything—through sun and sea, through the veins of the earth into root and leaf, into grain and fruit, into all women and all men. And each birth became forever an acceptance of splendor and each death a gift to the Great Mother."
>
> —JUNE BRINDEL[1]

There was a time when to be a woman was to be directly in the image of the Divine. There was a time when God was a Woman and Her spaciousness filled the vision and touched the hearts of every man, woman, and child who worshiped Her. She was called Goddess, Lady, Mother of All. Her manifestations were many: Huntress and Mistress of Animals, Lady of the Plants, Queen of Heaven and Earth, Creator, Sustainer, and Destroyer. It was She who created life and nourished it and She who deprived it and took it away. All things were subject to the Great Mother who was the origin and resource of every living thing and of the inanimate world as well.

The diversity and richness of Her images attest to a vision of Woman among the ancients that was spacious, complex, and multifaceted. This vision conveyed to feminine experience depth of meaning, awesome power, and profound value. So much that is lost, split off, devalued, or left unnamed in women's experiences today was once integrated into a vast vision of femaleness that was so valued, it was seen as holy. This included sexuality, menstruation, birthing, mothering, menopause, aging, and power, to name but a few areas in women's lives that were valued by Goddess-worshiping peoples in ancient times but that have been devalued or stereotyped in our own. To turn back to these ancient images, to try to reconstruct their meaning in their own times as best we can, and to dream them forward into new meaning for our own time deepens and enriches our experience of ourselves as women. The multiple faces of the feminine God expand our vision of what a woman is and offer us a broader possibility for reclaiming and naming our own experience. They also help us, by contrast, to identify more clearly the patriarchal vision of women inherent in our own cultural tradition and to determine for ourselves which aspects of that particular vision accurately comprehend our experience and which do not. This aids in the true naming of ourselves which is the central individuation task of women today.

The religion of the Goddess dates back to at least 10,000 B.C.E., and flourished for a subsequent 7,500 years, particularly among agricultural peoples in Southern Europe. Evidence of its original predominance in Africa, India, the Middle East, and the British Isles has also been documented. Around 3,500 B.C.E., the Goddess-worshiping peoples were infiltrated by patriarchal invaders from the North, Aryan peoples who moved down and across most of Asia and Europe, bringing with them the worship of a dominant, warring sky god, a we/they division of the world, and attitudes toward the feminine as subservient that have lasted to this day.[2]

Even after the invasions, which took place over several thousand years, some of the Goddess religion survived, coexisting with patriarchal religions such as Judaism and Hinduism or manifesting in distorted forms within patriarchal religion itself. By the time of classical Greece, many of the attributes and powers that once had characterized the Great Mother had been usurped by dominant male deities such as the sky-and-thunderbolt god Zeus, an Aryan import. The Great Mother's origins became obscured; Her tales were retold in distorted form. The feminine Deity, whom once even the gods were said to have acknowledged as Mother, was reimaged as subservient. She became consort, wife, sister, daughter to the male and, in the later Virgin Mary, Mother only to a son, to whom She is subordinate, a human vessel to the Divine, now imaged exclusively as masculine. Still She survived, through the persecution of Her priestesses by early Christianity, through the strict control of woman's "place" within and without the church that went so far as to kill women who deviated from this place during the Middle Ages[3]—the same church that just recently reaffirmed its pronouncement of women as unfit to be direct mediators of the Divine. Yet, unwittingly, the Catholic Church has also kept the Goddess alive; She lives on in pale versions of Herself, Her once-holy attributes appearing in stories of the lives of women saints,[4] and in the various images and ways of revering the Virgin Mary.[5] But, in these forms, She no longer represents the wholeness of women's experience nor does She offer a multiplicity of models for being a woman or a mother. She has been made small, confined to a few of Her attributes, divested of magnitude and power, overlaid with stereotypes of womanhood—as have the women whose lives still mirror Hers.

The last decade in particular has witnessed a resurgence of interest in the ancient Goddess from diverse quarters. Archaeologists, depth psychologists, artists, writers, ministers, priests, and historians have brought forth book after book on the Goddess and Her meaningfulness for our times. A "women's spirituality" movement has arisen, ranging in scope from those who want to unbury and revalue the feminine aspects of traditional religions such as Judaism and Christianity to those who wish to create anew ritual and worship drawn from the images and traditions of ancient times.[6] Therapists who work with dreams and other visionary material are seeing the appearance of numinous female figures, sometimes directly connected with the ancient images of the Goddess, in the material of people who have had no access to such imagery and would not consciously conceive of nor readily accept the concept of a "goddess."[7] Everywhere, individually and collectively, people are "waking up" to a new connection with a transpersonal and expanded view of the Feminine and finding new meaning and vitality in their lives because of it. For woman, this reconnection touches a profound hunger, a soul need to grow into and claim a Self that is bigger than the cultural dictates, that values *all* of her experience, and that gives a deeper and more authentic meaning to her life.

Carol Christ, a feminist theologian who has written extensively on women's spiritual quest, has suggested that whether we think of the Goddess as a personified Being or as energy that occurs within and between women, the image of the Goddess is an acknowledgement of female power, power not dependent on men nor derived from the patriarchal vision of women. It is an affirmation of the female body, a valuing of feminine will, and a recovery of the mother–daughter relationship in its larger context. Finally, it is a significant aspect of our feminine heritage, a heritage that has been unknown and lost to most of us but one that links us backward and forward to women across time and culture.[8] In other words, the Goddess reflects back to us what has been so missing in our culture: positive images of our power, our bodies, our wills, our mothers. To look at the Goddess is to remember ourselves, to imagine ourselves whole.

Before the shrinking of the Feminine was the Goddess—and all that is split in our own lives was in harmony in Hers.

She was profoundly in Her body. Her body itself was sacred. In the Old Religion, body and spirit were one. She was seen as substantial, as essentially embodied (Figure 1). Her thighs, Her belly, Her breasts were generous, Her physical strength apparent. We miss the beauty of such an image, we who have been taught to measure ourselves endlessly. Too fat, too thin, too flat, too wrinkled: Our bodies are never good, in themselves. We must deny our naturalness to see beauty.

What we learn to reject was once holy. What we learn to hide behind closed doors was once celebrated in the open. Blood was sacred to the Goddess—menstrual blood. Some of Her images were painted red between the legs. What some of us and many of our mothers learned to see as "the Curse" was once seen as the Blessing, women's particular creative magic. The blood that flows of itself and not from a wounding was thought to be the very source of life.[9] One early creation tale stated that when the Mother created man and woman, She made them from a mixture of Her menstrual blood and clay.[10] Moreover, every woman carried some of the Goddess's sacred substance and participated in Her ability to create life. Ancient peoples believed that pregnancy occurred when a woman "withheld" her blood, storing it up inside her until it formed a child who flowed out at birth. At menopause, when she withheld her magic blood for longer and longer periods and finally forever, her creativity became even more potent, creating no longer human infants but a feminine wisdom, which then flowed out to teach and guide the tribe.[11] Aging meant an accumulation of feminine wisdom deep within her, from whose richness she could draw to nourish the whole community with her knowledge. Thus the older woman became a "bigger" mother, moving beyond the care of her literal children to approximate more closely the Mother of All, in whose image she was made.

In addition to Her blood, pregnancy and birth were seen as sacred in the Goddess. She was pictured giving birth to animals, to children, to the world. Imagine an image of birthing on an altar, the blood and waters that the early church fathers subtracted from the Virgin's birthing of Christ once again present, restored to their previous numinous potency. Everything "natural" to woman had meaning, secular as well as spiritual, in the religion of the Goddess.

Her womb was especially emphasized. Image after image accentuates the pelvic triangle (Figure 2). This was the place of origin, this was the center of the world. Out of Her body all things came into being. Extending far beyond literal biological events, the womb was the essence of the Creative and creativity was female.

Her breasts! (Figure 3). What power was attributed to them, for they brought not only milk but life-giving rain.

In many cultures, the eyes of the Goddess were sacred (Figure 4). They had the power to stare down and mesmerize, as in the case of the Medusa, or to draw toward, to fascinate and compel. One archaeologist, after seeing dozens of figures in which the eyes repeatedly appeared over symbols of water, speculated that ancient people believed that at the center of the world, where the primal waters flow, are the Goddess's eyes.[12] Imagine Her gaze in the center of the Self, where the life flow begins. . . . What would it mean to be seen by Her? What of ourselves would we see reflected? We are taught not to really look at ourselves or each other. We are taught to look primarily through the eyes of men. We are taught to measure our images, our minds, our bodies in terms of whether and how much they will be "pleasing" to the other.

It is hard to be brief when speaking of the Goddess's sexuality. In our culture, the Divinity has gender but not sexuality; what is sexual is opposed to what is spiritual. In the Old Religion, this split that we are taught from early childhood on did not exist. Merlin Stone, in her book *When God Was a Woman*, writes, "In the worship of the female Deity, sex was Her gift to humanity. It was sacred . . . the act of sex was considered to be . . . so holy and precious that it was enacted within the house of the Creatress of heaven, earth, and all life. . . ."[13]

It wasn't just the sexual act that was holy. Her genitals were sacred (Figure 5) and were connected with a joyous self-celebration. Thus a poem about the Sumerian Goddess Inanna, written around the year 2000 B.C.E., relates:

> Inanna placed the shugurra, the crown of
> the steppe, on her head.
> She went to the sheepfold, to the shepherd.
> She leaned back against the apple tree.
> When she leaned against the apple tree,
> her vulva was wondrous to behold.
> Rejoicing at her wondrous vulva, the young
> woman Inanna applauded herself.[14]

In another poem, this radiant goddess sings explicitly of her sexuality:

> What I tell you,
> let the singer weave into song.
> What I tell you,
> let it flow from ear to mouth,
> let it pass from old to young:
> My vulva, the horn,
> the Boat of Heaven,
> is full of eagerness like the young moon.
> My untilled land lies fallow.[15]

Then She calls to Her lover, Dumuzi, directly:

> Then plow my vulva, man of my heart!
> Plow my vulva![16]

The image in Figure 5 comes from ancient Egypt. But, surprisingly, similar images appear in the architecture of some medieval English and Irish churches (Figures 6 and 7). Some of these figures, called *sheela-na-gigs* or *sheelas*, predate the churches they were part of; others don't. Not much is known about their meaning. They were believed to have curative and fertility powers and, as in much earlier Goddess worship, people touched and rubbed these figures.[17] Many were found in archways, so it was as if one would have to enter the church *through* Her.

We joke about "Mother Nature" (Figure 8). We've parodied in margarine commercials what was once holy: "It's not nice to fool Mother Nature!" boomed a voice, some years ago on television, when the person in the commercial discovered he or she was eating margarine instead of butter. In the Old Religion, the Deity was essentially at one with nature; nature and spirit were also not split off from each other. The Goddess was Lady of the beasts, of plants, of the earth, and of the heavens.

The moon was her special symbol: birth, death, and regeneration, all imaged vividly by the changes of the moon, were the essential expression of the feminine Deity. And all creatures that mirrored this were sacred to Her: the snake shedding its skin, the bull and cow with their crescent-shaped horns, the butterfly miraculously reborn out of its chrysalis coffin.

Moreover, She could become any one of Her creatures, take on the shape of a snake, a bull, or a tree (Figure 9). To be in the form of an animal or a plant was not a diminishment of the Divine but rather a further expression of Her qualities. Other animals were particularly sacred to Her. Birds spoke to Her and gave Her prophecies and She is often represented with bird companions (Figure 10) or as having bird attributes. Fish expressed Her connections with the depths and the primal waters. The original "mermaid," the figure so familiar to us from children's fairy tales, was once an image of the Goddess.

We label this *pantheistic.* To be seen as an animal in our culture is to be disdained. Like many little Adams, we believe we should dominate nature; we kill, we pollute, we uproot without replenishing. The bumper sticker popular among some environmentalist groups showing an image of the earth with the caption "Love Your Mother" hearkens back to a much earlier time, when such love was considered a spiritual imperative, when to violate nature was to desecrate the Great Mother. Then, even to cut down a single tree that was sacred to Her was to court severe punishment and possibly death.[18]

There are countless representations of the Goddess that directly portray Her as Mother (see Figures 11 and 12). It is important that, in this context, "Mother" is to be seen symbolically as well as literally. She was not only Mother as birth giver of animals, plants, and humans; She was Mother as Matrix, Origin, First Cause of all. Thus, She could be seen as Mother of the life force, of an earthquake, of smallpox, even as Mother of death. So, too, Her "child" was not only the literal child but also a symbol for all that flowed forth from Her and was dependent on Her. A song from a group of Colombian Indians quoted in Erich Neumann's book *The Great Mother* captures poetically the universality of the Goddess as Mother:

> The Mother of Songs, the mother of our
> whole seed, bore us in the beginning.
> She is the mother of all races and tribes.
> She is the mother of the thunder, the mother of the
> rivers, the mother of trees and all kinds of things.
> She is the mother of songs and dances.
> She is the mother of the older brother stones.
> She is the mother of the grain and the mother of
> all things.
> She is the mother of the younger brother
> Frenchmen and of the strangers.
> She is the mother of the dance paraphernalia
> and of all temples and the only mother we have.
> She is the mother of the animals, the only one,
> and the mother of the Milky Way. . . .
> She is the mother of the rain, the only one we have.
> She alone is the mother of all things—
> she alone.
> And the mother has left a memory in all the temples.[19]

As Mother, the Goddess is the birther, caretaker, and sustainer of all that She brings forth. She is the embodiment of maternal concern, protectiveness, nurturance, tenderness, and love. She bestows Her blessings, pours our Her nourishment, much as we expect Her human counterparts to do. But the Great Mother is not only benevolent and tender. She does

FIGURE 1
Venus of Willendorf, Austria, Paleolithic.
(Courtesy of Marburg/Art Resource.)

FIGURE 2
Mother-Goddess from Ur, 4000 B.C.E.
(Courtesy of Scala/Art Resource.)

FIGURE 3
Diana of Ephesos, Rome, 2nd century.
(Courtesy of Alinari/Art Resource.)

FIGURE 4
Eye Goddess, Tel Brak, Mesopotamia, 3000 B.C.E.
(Reproduced by courtesy of the Trustees of the British Museum.)

FIGURE 5
"Baubo" figure, Egypt, Ptolemaic Period.
(Courtesy of the National Museum, Copenhagen, Dept. of Near Eastern and Classical Antiquities, inv. no. 11725.)

FIGURE 6
Sheela-na-gig, Kilpeck, 12th century.
(Courtesy of the Royal Commission on the Historical Monuments of England.)

FIGURE 7
Sheela-na-gig, Oaksey Church, Wiltshire, 14th century.
Note elongated vulva.
(Courtesy of the Royal Commission on the Historical Monuments of England.)

FIGURE 8
Diana of Versailles (Lady of the Beasts), Rome,
4th century B.C.E.
(Courtesy of Alinari/Art Resource.)

FIGURE 9
Tree Goddess, Egypt, 600 B.C.E.
(Courtesy of the Museum of the Louvre, © Photos R.M.N.)

FIGURE 10
Aphrodite on a Goose, Boetia, Classical period.
(Courtesy of the Museum of the Louvre, © Photos R.M.N.)

FIGURE 11
Isis Suckling Horus, Egypt, 12th dynasty.
(Courtesy of Marburg/Art Resource.)

FIGURE 12
Snake Goddess, Greece, 6th century B.C.E.
(Courtesy of the Staatliche Antikensammlungen und Glyptothek, Munich, inv. no. 5289.)

FIGURE 13
Gorgon, Corfu, 6th century B.C.E.
(Courtesy of Scala/Art Resource.)

FIGURE 14
The Vulture Goddess Nekhbet, Egypt, 18th dynasty.
(Courtesy of the Metropolitan Museum of Art.)

FIGURE 15
The Goddess Sekhmet, Egypt, Empire Karnak.
(Courtesy of the Metropolitan Museum of Art,
Gift of Henry Walters, 1915 [15.8.3.].)

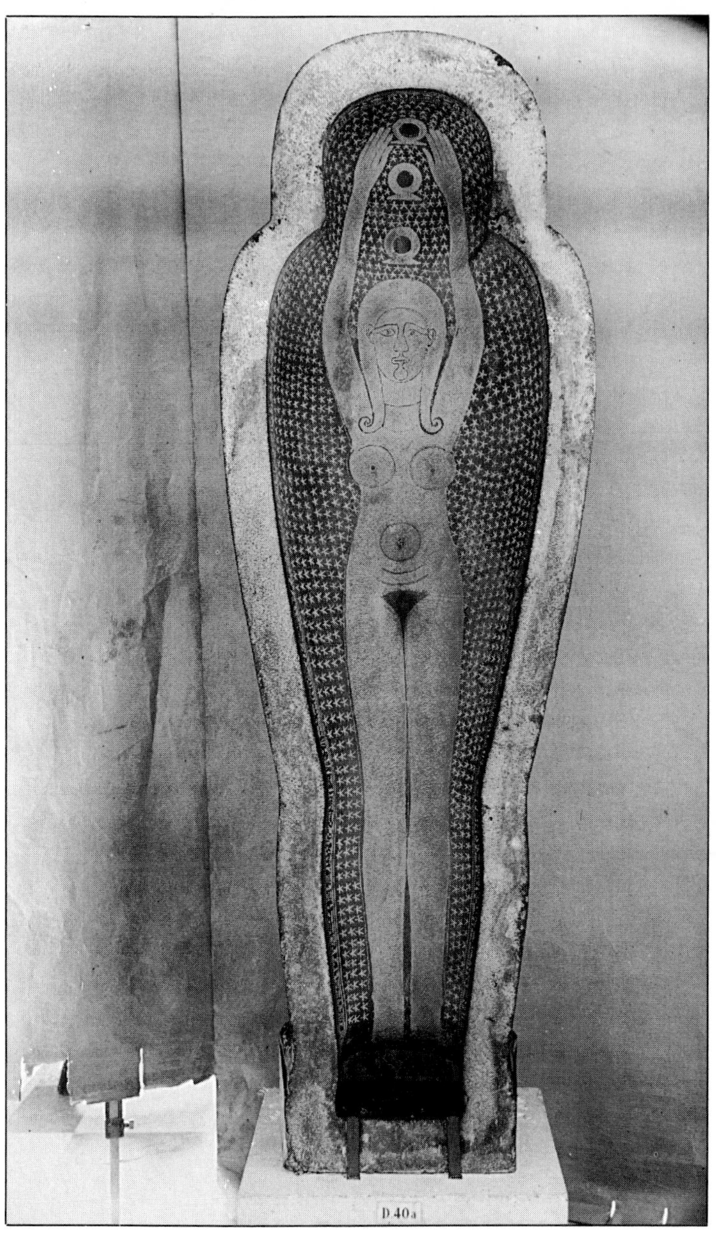


FIGURE 16
The Sky Goddess Nut on a Sarcophagus Lid
Interior, Egypt.
(Courtesy of Marburg/Art Resource.)

FIGURE 17
The Goddess Kali, India, contemporary, artist(s) unknown.
(In author's collection. Photo © 1989 Rachele Carlson.)

not only pour forth the sustenance upon which the world depends. To see Her fully, to image this great a Mother, is also to see Her as depriver and destroyer. She is the gorgon who terrifies and petrifies (Figure 13), the earth who is fertilized by blood, the vulture who feeds on the dead (Figure 14). She gives birth to Her children but She also devours them. She is the Goddess of Life but also the Goddess of Death.

The Great Mother is essentially bi-valent, embodying both a "good" and a "terrible" aspect. Even the most benevolent of Her images have a darker, more savage side or a destructive "sister."[20] Yet this ambivalence is not a static either/or; it expresses one of the most profound and deeply held beliefs of the Old Religion—that life is essentially a *process*, "becoming" instead of "being," and that this process follows a cyclical pattern that endlessly repeats itself. Just as autumn and winter inevitably follow summer and then give rise to a new spring, just as a decaying fruit produces from its dying the medium that enables the hidden seeds within it to sprout, so it was a "given" to the ancients that the Mother of All embodied this basic and implacable natural way. So the Goddess created life, sustained it, destroyed it, and took it back into Herself in death, only to recycle what She had killed back into new life once more.

The widespread vision of Her as a Triple Goddess also expressed the cycle of birth–death–rebirth. The original God-in-Three-Persons, the Goddess was believed to manifest both successively and simultaneously as Maiden, Mother, and Crone. As Maiden, She guarded and expressed the beginnings of life and its early development; in this aspect She was seen as a young girl or the Kore. Her Mother aspect referred not necessarily to the biological condition of having a child but connoted the fruition of life, its maturity; in this aspect, She was seen as a mature woman. As Crone, She was seen as most powerful of all, for it was the Crone, representing the aging and end of life, who made the link between life and death; in this aspect, She appeared as an old woman or skeletal hag.

But the destruction of life brought about by the Crone was also an initiation into Her most profound mystery: that, out of death, She would create new life. Thus were the Crone and the Maiden inextricably linked and the cycle repeated and ongoing. In Her triple form, the Goddess also bestowed a meaningfulness and even sanctity to each phase of a woman's life. Unlike our culture, which values only a woman's youthfulness, earlier cultures valued the aging woman. In the vision of the Old Religion, it was the Crone who carried the most wisdom and power.[21]

As Destroyer, the Goddess was truly terrifying, the savage, devouring, and ruthless Mother. Like the fairy tale witch who later represented Her, She used her children to feed Herself instead of nourishing them; Her own needs were foremost and had to be satisfied.[22] Sometimes, even She was pictured as going too far in Her savagery and special measures had to be taken to call Her back to Her milder and more benevolent self. In one ancient Egyptian tale, for example, the lion-headed goddess Sekmet (Figure 15), carrier of the scorching desert sun, goes on a rampage of killing the human desecrators of the sun god Ra. Carried away by Her righteous fury, She goes too far and threatens the extermination of the whole human race. The gods try to stop Her but She is entranced with Her own Death power and declares Her joy in it. They resort to tricking Her by strewing the battlefield with jugs of red beer. Thinking it is blood, She drinks it and is overcome by its effects. When She awakens, She has returned to Her more benevolent and contained self.[23]

As Killer, the Goddess is terrifying, but as Receiver of the Dead, She appears again as the loving and tender Mother, cradling death as She had also cradled life. Death is a return to Her. Ancient Egyptians expressed this beautifully by painting images of the Goddess on the interior of the lids of their sarcophagi (Figure 16) so it was as if the dead person was watched over by the Goddess. Other peoples expressed the same idea by burying their dead in fetal positions or placing them in womb-shaped jars. Death was received by the Mother, even as it was brought about by Her.

One of the goddesses still extant whose mythology and imagery vividly express the life-and-death fullness of the Great Mother is the Indian goddess Kali (Figure 17). This goddess is both modern and ancient. She predated Christ yet is still worshiped in India today. She is the patroness of thieves. She is the goddess of destruction and death; She wears a necklace of human heads and a belt of human hands. Hotly sexual and aggressive, She creates death and dances in the midst of it. She is worshiped on the cremation grounds. But, She is also the good and benevolent Mother who is nurturing and tender with Her children.[24] Ramakrishna, a spiritual leader in the late nineteenth century and one of Her greatest devotees, spoke of playing with Mother Kali and approaching Her as a much-loved child. A later devotee describes Her and suggests Her rich meaning: "She wears necklaces of gold and pearls, a golden garland of human heads, and a girdle of human arms. She wears a golden crown, golden ear-rings, and a golden nose-ring with a pearl-drop. She has four arms. The lower left hand holds a severed human head and the upper grips a blood-stained sabre. One right hand offers boons to Her children; the other allays their fear. The majesty of Her posture can hardly be described. It combines the terror of destruction with the reassurance of motherly tenderness. For She is the Cosmic Power, the totality of the universe, a glorious harmony of the pairs of opposites. She deals out death, as She creates and preserves. She has three eyes, the third being the symbol of Divine Wisdom; they strike dismay into the wicked, yet pour out affection for Her devotees."[25] The goddess Kali is a very full image of the Great Mother. She strikes terror into Her children, yet also comforts them and offers Her blessings. In Her, the primal forces of Life and Death exist together.

Among the myths still available to us, almost none depicts the Mother and Daughter relationship within its original Divine context. One exception is the Greek myth of the grain goddess Demeter and Her beloved daughter Kore, which is still readily accessible to us in the Homeric Hymn to Demeter.[26] The central focus of this myth is the rape and abduction of the maiden Kore by the Underworld brother of Zeus, the dread god Hades. Hades and Zeus were patriarchal imports into the previously dominant Mother religion. The myth, on one level, portrays the impact of the patriarchal invasions on the Goddess religion, poignantly picturing it as a wrenching separation of a positively bonded Mother and Daughter.[27] But in this myth the Mother isn't simply overcome: She fights back. The usually mild and tender Demeter waxes vicious in Her grief and rage and withdraws Her gift of grain. The farmers' fields lie barren. Zeus is deprived of the offerings of the first fruits of the harvest and human beings are threatened with starvation. No amount of cajoling persuades Demeter to relent, and finally Zeus has to give in. He restores the Maiden to Her Mother, although a last-minute trick of Hades commits Her to the Underworld. Thus She will divide Her time between Her Mother and the Lord of the Underworld, a partial triumph for each.

This myth is complex and multilayered but its key emotional aspect is of particular relevance here. Neither Mother or Daughter willingly collude with the forces of patriarchy. Demeter fights for Her daughter's return while Kore refuses to cooperate with Hades in the Underworld and longs for Her mother. Hades, as carrier of patriarchal values and masculine determination of what woman's "place" shall be, severs the primary bond between women and separates daughter from mother.

I think we know something about this separation. I think we especially know what it's like to be the Kore—torn from our roots, our home, our feminine heritage. We've lived in a spiritually alien world, filled with an unnameable homesickness[28] for something we've never known (for most of us have not had the original bond with a solid Demeter). And this homesickness, this longing for the lost Mother, comprises the archetypal core of the yearning of the unhealed child. From an archetypal perspective, it is our Selves we are longing for and a Mother as spacious and vast as our souls need. The myth suggests that the patriarchal rupture can be at least partly repaired with devotion, loyalty, and remembering across separation. For modern women, this requires rediscovering what has been lost and refinding an authentic connection to it.

Some women coming to the Goddess may find the most meaning in perceiving Her as transcendent, a Being "out there" to be approached in ritual, prayer, and worship. For these women, the Goddess becomes the origin and center of their lives and its reason for being. They may experience Her dialoguing with them in prayer or meditation or visiting them in visions or in dreams. They may experience themselves as "children of God," daughters of a Great Mother, and seek to serve Her in their daily lives. They may find profound meaning in their lives in the perception that they are "in Her image." Thus, an old woman may find reassurance and comfort in knowing that her body is still in the image of the Divine and look to discover the imprint of the Crone's wisdom in her mind and spirit. A middle-aged woman may recognize that she is now in the time of the Mother and seek out Her guidance to embody the energy and effort that are vital to bring her life to fruition. A young woman may see in the Maiden the beauty and exuberance of her own developing body and spirit and measure them not in terms of a culture that seeks to fix and encase her in this phase of her life but as a prefigurement of the fuller Mother and Crone that she will become.

For other women, the Goddess is not "out there" but "in here." These women perceive the feminine Deity as immanent, God-in-us, as forces and energies within and between women. Thus, we may see Her refusal to serve the patriarchy in a protest against nuclear weapons or a Take-Back-the-Night rally on a college campus.[29] We may find Her as Creatrix in ideas that inspire and spark us or honor Her as Destroyer and Rebirther when we feel the effects of a cleansing rage that tears down an old relationship but also clears the way for new growth. She may appear as Law in the necessity to learn how to care for a sick child even when we may not want to and it is a great inconvenience. We may experience Her as Huntress in the fierce confrontation by another and, recognizing Her energy in the sharp words and intensive probing, submit to Her arrows until they hit the mark and our own hidden truth can be exposed, stripped of defenses like a wounded animal. We may find Her as Mother and Maid when we commit ourselves to support and develop a nascent ability, a new project, an unrealized dream.

Whether we perceive Her as transcendent or immanent or both, the Goddess in Her rich and varied forms allows us to make new meaning of our experiences as women. She offers us a vision of being female that extends far beyond the limits of our cultural image, and reclaims to deep significance all that has been split off or lost. Through Her, we can reclaim the life of our bodies, our self-generative creativity, the meaningfulness of the entire cycle of our lives from childhood to old age, find a new connectedness to nature, even come to understand our rage and destructiveness as balance points for our capacities to nurture and to love. Through Her we are reborn into connection with the "container" for our lives that the unhealed child in us is crying for. The Goddess visions us anew, outside of the eyes of patriarchy.

But Her images and stories also enable us to identify and name that which is already there, experiences that we may apprehend inside ourselves but have no words with which to express them. Many women, for example, experience a connection within themselves between sexuality and spirituality that they have no words for. Turning to the culture for understanding, they may find themselves labeled "blasphemous" or "weird" or "obscene." Yet even if they believe these labels, they may continue to feel that something precious is being misperceived, something significant and *real* in their experience is not being seen. This is true in so many areas of women's lives. It is part of the reason we need to create a new language, as Adrienne Rich suggests,[30] to name our experience authentically, and why we need increasingly to risk more in revealing ourselves to each other. I once taught a class on "women's experiences of power" in which each woman (including myself) had silently vowed to herself before class that she would not reveal her real experience of "positive power." Each woman feared she would be seen as "crazy" by the others and be faced with that painful experience of isolation in not being understood, that isolation we know so well. When one woman courageously made the leap of self-revelation, enabling the rest of us to follow suit, we discovered an incredible congruence of experience. Almost every one of us had experienced deep moments of becoming a "channel" for Power bigger than ourselves but none of us knew how to name these experiences, nor did we imagine that they might be shared by other women.

There are other areas of transpersonal experience in women's lives that are difficult to name and so often go unshared. In pregnancy and childbirth, for example, some women are gripped by a Life-and-Death drama that totally destroys an old ego sense of "being in control" and initiates them into far more than the experience of having to cope with a new baby. They may find themselves face to face with the Mother as Creator and Destroyer, manifesting in irrational terrors or visions or dreams.[31] Yet there is little available from the culture to guide them through this initiation into deeper layers of themselves and the transpersonal dimension of the bi-valent Feminine. Here, a knowledge of the Goddess and Her powers can be of enormous help in these bigger-than-human experiences.

Dreaming Her forward by being open to new experiences and new expressions of the Goddess are also vital tasks for our time. Thus we participate in creating new myth and new meaning. To this end, we may also need to draw from the meanings and beliefs of the past and recreate them in the present on another level, in language and understanding more relevant to our own time. We know, for example, that menstrual blood does not coagulate to literally create a baby; the facts of conception are known to us. We also know that we don't literally control the menstrual flow. We know we don't have the ability to release or contain it at will. Some of us may remember hearing of other myths about menstrual power. We may recall an ancient belief that if menstrual blood were mixed with earth, it could fructify a field. Or we may remember the basis of various menstrual taboos: the belief that to look on the face of a menstruating woman was to risk being paralyzed or killed and that therefore women had to be sent away from the community during their time of magic so that they would do no harm.[32] We know that our blood does not have the capacity to fertilize or kill. Thus, for us, the myths of blood power and creation from blood are not literally true.

But if we look at the myths of the powers of menstrual blood symbolically and psychologically instead of literally, we come up with some radical ideas about feminine creativity and see a new angle on the answer to that tired old question, "Why aren't there more creative women?" Looking at blood power symbolically, we could say: There is a power in what flows from within us. What flows out of us periodically as an expression of feminine nature has the power to fructify, to facilitate life around us or to freeze it, to kill it. This reflects Nature Herself, which both engenders and supports life and destroys it. We could name this as primal feminine power. Looked at psychologically and symbolically, our magic "flow" could be a flow of words, of feeling, of passion, judgment, or sexuality. But in our culture only one kind of consequence is "supposed" to come about from our flow. In our culture, there is a great emphasis on women being facilitators; we are taught that our flow should be used to support and fertilize life only. And we are punished and feared if our power is used to limit or prevent others, to "freeze them in their tracks."

The ancient myths also suggest that if we choose to withhold our flow, to retain it and store it up, we have the power to create new life *by ourselves*. Psychologically speaking, this is an image of profound, willful introversion and creation not dependent on connection with a man. The radical piece of this is that this myth suggests that withholding, refusing to flow, keeping our magic for ourselves, is the source or one source of feminine creativity. Refusing to flow out *makes new life.*

This is very taboo in our society. In a patriarchal society, women are supposed to flow out all the time, to nourish, support, and use their magic to be of service to others, especially to children and to men. Others depend on that flow as if it were lifeblood and yet it is also devalued, its power deprecated. A woman who spends her life serving a man, a household, and children is seen as "just a housewife."

Many women feel a taboo around keeping some of their flow for themselves or refusing to flow (claiming the right to "just say no"). This taboo is what underlies the huge concerns expressed in therapy by so many women about "being selfish." "Do I have a right to have something for myself separate from the family?" "Do I have a right to have for myself if it means depriving someone else?" The right to space and time for herself, to nourish herself instead of always nourishing others, to use her skills and gifts and passion—her "magic"—for *herself* has been taboo in our society. For some women, even having their own thoughts and images are seen as somehow illicit and dangerous. Intentional introversion and "holding back her flow" are seen in our culture as "selfish" and "unnatural."

Yet the myths of blood power don't posit an either/or situation. What flows out is periodic; it is not all the time but occurs at somewhat regular intervals. Retaining the flow to create new life also happens only periodically though it lasts for nine months (interestingly, the time it often takes women to complete their projects). Nothing is static in the Feminine. "Storing up" and introversion are not ultimate endpoints but only one part of a cycle. After we have held our magic in long enough, gestated it until it takes on new form, it too flows forth. What we have created flows back into the world.

The myths and imagery of the Goddess provide us with

rich material with which to symbolically refertilize our lives. As Goddess, She is mirror to the feminine Self and addresses the hunger in every woman for connection with that Self. Seen as Mother, however, She can lead us down additional paths of meaning. Seeing Her as the Great Mother can help us put our personal mothers in perspective, expand our vision of "maternal" behaviors, and broaden the concept of being nurtured to include input from many different kinds of women. It may also bring deep reassurance and self-understanding to women who are mothers or who wish to be and who seek to discover how to cope with and how to comprehend what it means to carry an archetype.

# 8

# THE GREAT MOTHER AS ARCHETYPAL DYNAMIC IN PERSONAL EXPERIENCE

The Great Mother is more terrible, more powerful, and more expansively benevolent than the "smaller" mothers who raised us. Our mothers are merely human beings, not as "great" or vast or powerful as the Mother of the legends, the images, the worship of ancient times. Nevertheless, our personal mothers carry aspects of the Goddess, and identifying these aspects helps us understand what we have already experienced, both positively and negatively. It also helps us begin to grasp what we still need in order to come closer to a wholeness of the Feminine.

Erich Neumann, in his work *The Great Mother*, articulates two "characters" of the Goddess: the elementary character and the transformative character. Each character consists of behavior, themes, and images that delineate the nature of the Goddess but that are also readily found in partial form in our experiences of our human mothers. Each of these characters is bi-valent, having a benevolent and a terrible form.[1] An examination of these two aspects of the Goddess helps us identify those places in our personal experiences of our mothers that are also "windows" into the Great Mother. Discovering how the Goddess comes through our mothers reframes our personal experience and makes possible a larger context of meaning.

In Her elementary aspect, the Mother's energy is essentially conservative. She holds to Herself all to which She has given birth. In this aspect, She isn't interested in fostering the independence of Her child or its individuality, but in keeping it connected with Her.[2]

This aspect is expressed positively as maternal preservation, protection, and nourishment. The positive elementary mother is a good "container," a shelter from danger and threat, a conserving womb that carries the child within boundaries while it grows. The Goddess as Vessel, as Cow Mother nourishing all life with Her milk, as Womb pouring forth grain, as fertile Mother Earth expresses the positive elementary character. So, too, Her symbolic connections with cave, house, temple, and cradle.[3] The Goddess in this aspect of Herself is the quintessential "Good Mother," the origin, creator, and sustainer of Her child's life. Her relationship to Her child is defined by connectedness. The child is bound to her Mother not only by love and dependence but by identification. She is essentially her Mother's "offspring" and, profoundly, positively, "in Her image." Some sculptures of Demeter and Kore, for example, depict Mother and Daughter as mature, full-bodied women, essentially indistinguishable except for the different symbols they carry in their hands. This kind of connectedness is expressed mythologically when the child of the Goddess has a name that is merely a variant of Her own (a pattern that appears in human form as well; my own mother's name is a variant of my grandmother's and I have a friend whose name means the "little" version of her mother's).

The Goddess in Her positive elementary aspect merges with much of our cultural ideal of the "good mother" and is perhaps most familiar to us as conscious experience in the positively bonding mother whose care, nourishment, and affection literally sustain her daughter's life as a child, and remain a psychic matrix to her as an adult. "Going home to mother," literally or psychically, is a positive experience in this context and, indeed, the good mother carries the archetypal sense of "home": the sourceground, the origin, the place we can always return to for a sense of belonging and the reassurance of shelter and care. Crystal Eastman's experience of her mother as origin and shelter vis-à-vis a temporarily alienating world is a good example of this. The emphasis on connection through identification or similarity that characterizes this aspect of the Goddess is humanly reflected in the little girl dressing up in her mother's clothes, playing "Mommy," or packing her "briefcase" just like her businesswoman mother. (I remember, with humor and affection, a time when my three-year-old daughter finished everything on her plate at dinner, looked over at me, and exclaimed with satisfaction, "There! I ate my supper just like a woman!") This type of connection is equally expressed in the adult daughter who genuinely admires her mother and feels good about those aspects of herself that are "just like Mom."

Some women did not experience the positive elementary mode in their relationships with their mothers or had far too little access to it. For these women, subsequent experiences of this with other women as lovers, friends, mentors, therapists, or even women in dreams can be extremely healing and come with all the fullness of the archetype. As a therapist I have worked with several women who were abused or neglected by their mothers and knew nothing of "positive bonds." With these women, often the smallest kindness or concern on my part, the most ordinary protectiveness, was experienced as hugely healing, like extraordinary "food" reaching deep into the needs of a hungry and hurting child. Such experiences of a numinous, nourishing Mother can also appear in visions or in dreams. One woman, whose mother had been extremely withholding, self-serving, and had often abandoned her daughter to potentially dangerous situations, came into therapy terrified of having to come to terms with her often chaotic and tumultuous childhood. Over and over, in the beginning of therapy, she had dreams of war and near annihilation, often in the setting of her childhood home. In one such dream, she and her boyfriend were hiding in a closet with the enemy all around. The dreamer relates:

> The worst scene was when Bill and I were in a closet. The enemy was in the building we were in and this was our only place to hide; it wasn't a good one. We covered ourselves with clothes as best we could and waited. A woman came into the closet—she saw us but said nothing. Instead she tried to cover us up better so that we wouldn't be found—she also gave us each some sugar water. We knew that she had probably been taken prisoner and that this sugar solution was the only food that she had been given and she was sharing it with us. We knew too that if they found us, they would kill her for not telling them we were there. None of us said a word—we only looked at each other—but Bill and I felt deep gratitude toward this woman and were deeply moved by her help.

The woman in the dream does not obviously bear the earmarks of the Goddess; indeed, she appears to be a victim herself, or so the dreamer assumes. But her impact on the dreamer's consciousness was larger than life and transformative. The dreamer was profoundly moved by this woman and woke in a state of awe. For another woman to risk her life to protect and nourish her was unimaginable; she had never experienced this kind of care or self-sacrifice. The dream woman seemed to emanate an aura of magic and healing; even years later, the dreamer was moved by the memory of this image of care. To sugar water, she associated a time when she had been a nurse's aide and had been asked to sit with a dying old woman and moisten her lips with glycerin and water; she thought this was to get some kind of nourishment into her. She also thought she had heard that sometimes premature babies were fed a sugar solution for nourishment. Dimly she recognized, from both her associations and the situation in the dream itself, that it was her own endangered life that the dream woman was trying to protect and feed, a life that had been rendered nearly unviable psychologically and that had been driven into hiding by the depth of her mother's pathology. At the time of the dream, the dreamer could not take in real nourishment from other people, especially from women. She hid both her neediness and fragility beneath a shield of self-sufficient bravado. Gradually, she learned to trust her therapist and then other women and to take in precisely those maternal qualities that had not been present in her personal mother: the protectiveness and nurturance of the positive elementary Mother that came to her first in a dream.

The conservation and "holding" nature of the elementary aspect of the Mother are not always positive. This aspect is also expressed and experienced in negative form. Negatively valanced, "holding fast" to Herself becomes holding back, fixating, refusing separation, and possessiveness. "Containing," in this light, becomes constriction and incarceration. In Her most extreme form, the negative elementary Mother takes back what She has given birth to, assimilating it to Herself or devouring it. The Goddess as Child-Eater, as petrifying Gorgon, as Lion and Vulture, as the hungry Earth that must be fed with corpses expresses the negative elementary character. The symbols connected with this aspect include the underworld, devouring animals, the coffin or grave as "container," and the image of the vagina dentata.[4]

In human form, this aspect of the Goddess is experienced in the binding mother who cannot allow her daughter to be different from herself, or support her desires for autonomy. It is also expressed in the mother who merges psychologically with her daughter and sees her daughter's personality and accomplishments only in terms of how they reflect on her. One element in matrophobia, seen here from an archetypal rather than a personal or cultural perspective, is fear of being assimilated to the mother, dissolving into her or being "just like her," no longer separate, individual, oneself. The negative elementary Mother is the archetypal image behind many of the fears that women have around their personal mothers or other women, fears of being devoured, overpowered, assimilated, fixated, or pulled into some kind of regressive bind. When these fears take on irrational proportions, far beyond the actual human powers of the woman in question, it is this aspect of the Goddess that has been activated in the psyche.

For a growing child or adult woman to experience herself as being in the image of the positive elementary mother is, on the human level, a pleasurable and reassuring experience. For this to be experienced on the level of the Goddess, to be "just like *Her*," conveys a profound sense of meaning and value to one's life and one's womanhood; it may even take on mystical proportions. Thus, one woman who discovered in therapy that her deepest and innermost self had survived intact despite a childhood of severe emotional abuse from her family envisioned herself as having been loved and protected by the Goddess. Coming to feel that her deeper self was like a mirror of the Goddess's imprint upon her, she believed that her particular spiritual quest was to find how to live that imprint more fully and visibly, how to draw out and have the courage to embody that Goddess-given self.

For the daughter who is faced with the negative elementary aspect of the mother, the message that conveys "You are in my image" is both noxious and frightening. On the personal level, with her mother or other women, she experiences this as a dangerous "glue" or a deindividualizing of herself that she has to fight off or deny. On an archetypal level, such experiences can take on truly terrifying proportions, coming through in nightmares of devouring female figures or death fears; it is as if the Universe itself seeks to devour or annihilate her personal being. "Maternal," in this context, is terrifying and connected with dissolution of the self.

Neumann's conception of the second major character of the Goddess is captured succinctly in a contemporary chant: "She changes everything she touches, and everything she touches, changes."[5] In Her transformative aspect, the Great Mother promotes development, emphasizes independence, and stimulates transformation in Her child and the universe that She governs.[6] In this dimension, process and change are all and supplant the emphasis on bonding and sameness that is held by the elementary Mother. The stability and conservation of the elementary Mother are offset by the "perpetually becoming" that the transformative Mother in Her essence brings about.

This, too, can be positive or negative. In Her positive form, the transformative Mother promotes growth through guidance toward autonomy or through challenge and stimulation. It is She who inspires and entrances, bringing about positive changes of consciousness as well as of physical well-being. She is most familiar to us, perhaps, as the fairy godmother in children's stories whose appearance presages the granting of wishes and much-desired transformations. But She is also the Goddess as Muse, Lady of the Magic Cauldron, Moon Goddess, Lady of the Plants and Lady of the Beasts, Physician and Healer, Initiator into Mystery. She too is nourishing, but here the emphasis is on the change of form that Her nourishment brings about, and Her food is often magical or supernatural.[7] Moreover, She goes further than the elementary form of the Mother and teaches Her children how to exist beyond Her immediate gifts. Thus the goddess Demeter, bestower of the grain, was also said to have taught humanity the art of agriculture, enabling people to go beyond their passive dependence on Mother Nature's provisions and to plant and provide for themselves.

We see this in human form in the mother who can carry a positive bond with her daughter but who also supports and facilitates her autonomy. The positive transformative Goddess appears in Her human counterpart's extensive efforts to teach skills and convey knowledge to her daughter that will help her child grow beyond her into a competent and self-sufficient adult.[8] The domestic lives of many adult women are rooted in the teachings of their mothers. Baking, cooking, sewing, gardening (all essentially transformational activities), household economics and home management, child care, the mediation of relationships within and beyond the family—all those traditionally "feminine arts" that our culture ludicrously refuses to define as real "work"—have most often been passed down from mother to daughter. So, too, the psychological development that such skills require: the creation and maintenance of order, the capacity to handle multiple tasks simultaneously, the self-discipline to sublimate one's own needs and impulses to the benefit of the whole, and the empathic comprehension of the needs and abilities of several people simultaneously, each of whom is at a different stage of development. In our times, the mother increasingly mediates the world outside the home as well; she may actively support her daughter's intellectual interests, instruct her in self-assertion, the ability to network, and other skills that are vital to her well-being in the outer world. And, in the essence of the positive transformative spirit, she may encourage her daughter to grow beyond her, pursuing desires that the mother doesn't share and taking risks beyond those the mother was able to take in her own life. Through her mother's support, the daughter may feel inspired to greater achievement and personal expansion of her individual self with "no strings attached." We experience this aspect of the mother in other relationships as well, with women who serve us as mentors, role models, teachers, healers, and spiritual guides.

The negative transformative Mother also promotes growth and independence but brings them about through negative means: rejection, deprivation, attack, or abandonment. Such experiences can also challenge their recipients and stimulate new development, in addition to the hurt and damage they may inflict. On the Goddess level, this is often pictured in Her withdrawal from the land of the living (often to descend into the underworld),[9] or in Her appearance as Bringer of Scourge and Disease or as the Death Goddess who strips, kills, and dismembers the initiate to propel her into consciousness of the "other side."[10] In terms more familiar to us, we see Her as the wicked stepmother in fairy tales who persecutes the good child and sends her far from home and family to live by her own resources.

This aspect of the Mother teaches us that negative experience can also elicit positive growth. As disease can compel the body to produce vital and necessary defenses, sometimes even resulting in immunity to further attack, so the Goddess sometimes appears to infect Her children with trials and tribulations to innoculate them against Her own evil, to compel them to grow beyond their passive dependence on Her "good side" and to fight Her and stand up to Her instead. In this way She both challenges and strengthens the human ego. This mixture of positive and negative in the Goddess is a radically different conception of the Divine than the image of the all-good God we are used to, but accurately reflects our experience of life and lends depth and meaning to the mixture we encounter in Her human counterparts.

We encounter the negative transformative Mother in the "banishing" human mother who promotes the precocious independence of her daughter but cannot allow a dependent bond. We find Her in the drunk, crazy, or abusive mother who cannot or will not attend to her daughter's needs or, more mildly, in the momentary lapses of care in a mother who is sick, preoccupied with her own life, or otherwise "absent" temporarily. Such experiences throw us back on ourselves. We are forced to develop internal resources or the courage to move beyond our maternal experiences and seek help and nurturance from without. In addition, it is often in the areas of maternal deprivation that we as daughters are compelled to develop our greatest gifts and sensitivities. I have worked with several women, for example, who were never touched by their mothers, and became body therapists in later life. In my own life, it was undoubtedly my grandmother's psychosis and its ravaging effects on our bond that shaped my capacity for empathy and participation with suffering others and determined my early ambition to become a psychotherapist. Given the choice, I would still not elect to go through that experience, to suffer the terror and abandonment I felt nor to watch someone deeply loved be eaten alive by untreated illness. Nevertheless, the effects of this experience with my grandmother engendered many of the qualities and capacities I value deeply as an adult woman today. Even the mother's death can sometimes have a transformative effect on her daughter. In some women it brings to a close a fruitless, negative dependence on the mother's approval and disapproval and forces the unhealed child to at last look elsewhere for her fulfillment.[11]

To make meaning of such traumatic experiences is not to condone abuse or to trivialize destruction and suffering. Unlike the Goddess, who appears to mirror raw Nature in Her mixture of benevolence and cruelty, we human beings have a moral imperative to attempt to be responsible and to channel as constructively as we can the forces and primal impulses that course through us. But trauma and suffering occur, at the hands of our mothers and our gods, as well as in other aspects of our lives. To find frameworks we can use to make meaning of such experience enables us to rise above a one-sided despair that would have us give up on life; it also helps us face with more depth and perceptiveness the mixture of good and evil that most of us repeatedly experience as reality.

As archetypal image and as spiritual reality, the Great Mother carries in Her fullness the quaternity of Her aspects. In the deepest and most developed representations of the Goddess, positive and negative elementary aspects coexist in creative tension and balance with positive and negative transformative ones. In the human mother, however, these energies are more likely to be partially manifest and one-sided and in need of balance from without. The emotional thrust of the unhealed child is especially attuned to this need to balance, for usually what the unhealed child in us is searching most for is the mother we *didn't* have. Our task vis-à-vis this is twofold. On the one hand, we need to take the unhealed child's needs for compensatory experiences very seriously and recognize them as the basis of a spiritual quest for the wholeness of the Mother and the wholeness of ourselves. But we need also to bring to this the adult apprehension that the fullness of the Mother is beyond the capacity of one human being to manifest. Thus we must gently wean our inner children away from their fixations on our personal mothers and the demand that our mothers provide for all of our needs, and teach that wounded part of us to seek its healing in relationship with other women and in inner experience as well as with the personal mother. On the other hand, we must also help our wounded selves make sense of what we have already experienced and to penetrate it to the depths of its meaning where it too can be acknowledged as part of the Mother's truth and a contribution to our growth.

The need for compensation does not lie in one direction only. The unhealed child within us is usually seeking those positive experiences that will balance and assuage her negative ones. But the woman whose experience of her mother has been largely positive may also be in need of compensation for her further growth. Many adolescents who have been well nourished by their mothers act this out instinctively by suddenly accusing them of trying to hold them back and run their lives. Even if the baffled mother has no such designs on her daughter's life, the appearance of the negative elementary mother in her daughter's image of her at this point creates the necessary noxiousness against which the daughter can push to wrest herself free of her own dependency and separate from her mother. Sometimes, when that separation has been truly accomplished, the positive bond can be acknowledged again, transmuting from its childhood form into a mutual supportiveness as adults. Similarly, an adult daughter who was never subjected to abandonment and deprivation as a child may need to encounter those experiences later in life in order to discover what, within her, can stand for herself entirely alone when she is not being nurtured or supported from without. Such compensations for the childhood experience may come about through other women or as appearances of the Goddess in vision and in dreams.

But the Goddess does not always appear only to compensate the experiences we have had with our mothers. Sometimes She also appears to lend new dimensions and depth to those experiences, and teaches us a deeper perception and meaningfulness than our conscious minds already know.

Amy, the second-generation matrophobic daughter we met

in Chapter 5,[12] came into therapy in her early twenties consciously disdaining her mother's life of "staying home and having babies." What was most important to her was to develop her personal creativity and make it the basis of a thriving career, but she found this extremely difficult to do. She could always get started but never carry through. Amy believed that to be a creative person, she had to either be connected with a powerful man or be like a man herself; being female was a considerable hindrance to her goals. Several months into therapy, she had the following dream:

> It is known that this is the day that Christ is coming. There are radio announcements that everyone is gathering on a hill to watch the sky. I exit the house and as I am exiting, I grab a dusty book from a bookshelf. I don't know why I have done this but I make a point to look at this book as I know this will be important. It is a spiritual novel I read once and I pause for a moment to remember the message of this book—the SELF. I hear other people slowly climbing up to the top of the hill. We are all under the stars waiting. I notice as I begin to hear women's voices that we are all women gathered here. Then a wave of energy rushes back and forth through the crowd and I hear cries—cries of women giving birth and cries of children being born. I turn around in every direction and always there is one more woman who joins in. I am amazed. Right before I wake up, I realize that all the while we were looking up, it has been right here. That Christ is amongst us and it has to do with children and more so—the rebirth of women.

Amy woke from the dream filled with awe and knowing it was a "big" dream yet she felt baffled by its imagery. Having babies meant "losing your center forever," "being trapped." Consciously, the "savior" she was waiting for was the bigger-than-life "spiritual" man through whose power and status, she believed, she would realize her own ambition and creative promise. The seeds of a rich imagination and the urgency to bring them forth lay deep within her, yet, as the dream suggests, she was perpetually "looking in the wrong place" for what would enable it. Time after time, she projected all of her value onto a seemingly creative and powerful man, only to then go "empty," and ultimately feel used by him. Often she *was* used, latching onto severely narcissistic men who wanted nothing more from her than the mirror for their own grandiosity that her idealization of them and willingness to empty herself out in their presence provided. Yet, by herself, Amy was "only a woman" and women, in her estimation, had no value or power of their own.

Believing this, she could only get started with her creative ideas and projects, then passively wait for the man who would notice and enable their development. She lacked the capacity to carry her dreams through to fruition and to do the active, assertive work of bringing them forth into the world to gather the help and support they deserved. Ultimately, Amy thought so little of herself as a woman that her ego could not sustain her creative impulses. Thus, the appearance of the Self, and its attempt to joggle her consciousness and point it in another direction.

The qualities of feminine creativity that Amy's mother concretized into having babies were precisely what her daughter needed on another level to bring to her creative impulses. Symbolically speaking, being pregnant and giving birth are images of patiently gestating the growing life within, tending it to fruition, and then "birthing" it into the world, doing the hard, exertive "labor" needed to make it real and bring it forth.[13] Far from losing the center, giving birth in this sense means *becoming* the center of active, intensive effort to bring one's inner life into outer, incarnated being. For Amy, this meant staying with her own ideas instead of giving them over to the man or nurturing his creativity; it meant seeing her ideas through to completion and learning to be assertive enough to draw attention to her work and make the contacts that would help get it publicized.

Amy's dream also suggests that this is a collective issue for women and a collective process, though ultimately done by each individual. Amy was astonished to discover that other women had the same issues she did. She was even more amazed when she began to awaken to the interests and concerns of the feminist movement and to find supportive female friends who would help her learn to network effectively, and enable her work to be known. She had always seen women as merely "Adam's ribs," deriving their vitality and power from a man.

What is striking about the dream is that it takes precisely what was most loathsome to Amy in her experience of her mother and transposes it to its transpersonal form. Thus to go beyond concrete thinking about the Feminine and "remythologize" it brings in another layer of meaning. What can be concretized on a biological level into having a child can also be realized on a spiritual level as bringing forth the inner child of one's imagination and dreams. Either can be a deeply meaningful process. Both are contained as possibilities within the larger, transpersonal meaning of the birth-giving Womb.

Amy's dream does not "fill out" her mother experience by bringing in a compensatory image. Instead, it transposes the image already known to another level of meaning. Another transposition of the personal mother experience to the Goddess level and new meaning appears in the dream of Rosa, a woman in mid-life who came into therapy after the breakup of a thirty-year marriage:

> We're (all women) doing a show about fashion modeling. Each woman has gotten together an outfit. And there is a play about it. We ad-lib the play into existence during rehearsal. I manage to put things together for my role in the play in such a way that it synchronizes with the concept and works in with the others and enhances the play. And I'm told that I was the only one who got an *A* in my research (research for another project apart from the play). I add up my grades, 4 *A*s and a *B*+, and I think that's pretty incredible. Suddenly it's the night of the performance and my notes are still not written for the dialogue. I have too many props; the stage layout is unfamiliar. I can't remember the details of the rehearsal

(which supposedly must be duplicated). There's lots of activity in the dressing room a few minutes before the performance. I feel really scattered. I keep trying to remember the rehearsal. One or two members of the cast have not shown up.

Now my mother arrives in the dressing room dressed in black with a big black and white chain of primitive, bulky polished stones around her neck. She's made up and "dressed to kill," wearing a shiny black bird's wing (crow's or blackbird's) on her head like a hat. She says she has a present for me. I feel a wave of fury and resentment that she should come here and hang back from her. The present is sweet moist perfume which she squirts in a blast all over the dressing room. I ask her to leave. She does. But I feel her entrance has taken the vitality out of the enterprise. I have a faint sense of dread. Now I become even more apprehensive about the performance. The lights, stage—everything seems out of focus. I have too many props for the modeling sequence in my hand and can't seem to give any of them up. I'm scribbling notes for the dialogue and almost miss my cue. Someone tells me to come in at the center entrance instead of the side one. I do it. I don't ask why. The stage is too small. Lights blinding. I feel everything depends on me but I'm not 'in' the part. Through a fog of concern and confusion, I give my speech a little too soon—or too late. Someone tries to cover for me, to cue me. I can't hear. To recoup, I begin to go into the modeling sequence. I walk down toward the footlights with a frozen smile. At the apron I turn and almost lose my balance.

Afterwards there is a party for all the women in the play at a luxurious suburban house. We're being quartered by the fashionable hostess on different floors of the house. In the small bedroom I'm ushered into, I apologize for having wrecked the scene by my errors and by trying to remedy them. The four or five women in the room agree I goofed. I hate the clothes, the snobbery. I don't belong here. A territory inhabited by bourgeois women—silky, soft lights, expensive furni-

> ture, dozens of rooms, boudoirs. I feel out of place and really despise the whole oppressive environment.

The metaphors of "being on stage" and performing were consciously familiar to this woman. She frequently had described her prior life as being just a "performance," full of superficial, materialistic values and an overwhelming need to please. She described a fashion show as "doing something for appearance, an ego investment; one acts for public approval." This and the reference to "getting good grades" refer also to her previous mode of functioning. Then, her predominant concern had been to make sure she "looked good," no matter how she felt, and was approved of by everyone, especially her husband and his friends. This dream appeared on the occasion of a strong temptation to relapse back into this persona and its values, but the considerable, courageous work she had done in therapy to become more authentic was reflected in the dream; she just couldn't pull the performance off anymore. What surprised her is that her mother, whom she had experienced very negatively in her upbringing, facilitates the "undoing" of her persona which her dream ego resists but which she very much wanted and was working toward consciously.

Rosa experienced her mother as a dominant, uncaring, aggressive woman. In the dream, she appears in Goddess guise and on the side of the aspect of her daughter's ego that was consciously striving for transformation. She appears "dressed to kill" and, in fact, does take the life out of the show. The necklace she wears is connected to Kali, for when Rosa tried to hone in on the image more clearly, it appeared as a necklace of teeth or, alternatively, had a small human being dangling from it. The crow or black bird's wing she wore as a hat had particular personal meaning to the dreamer as well as striking archetypal meaning. For Rosa, it recalled to mind a recurring image she had experienced in her early twenties, when she felt she was suffering a breakdown. She had felt filled with rage and murderous toward her mother then, and every night had experienced a dark wing like a crow's coming down on her just before she went to sleep, which had terrified her. On a transpersonal level, the crow is also connected with death and destructiveness; it is sacred to the Black Crone who sometimes appears in its shape.[14]

In the dream, Rosa's mother wears the hat of killer rage and aggressiveness. She brings her "gift" of death; with her transformative perfume, she drains the life out of her daughter's fake persona, making it impossible for her to go back to that previous adaptation. Thus the negative transformative Mother "kills" for the sake of new life, and supports the developing ego. On a transpersonal level, this suggests that the Death Goddess sometimes functions as that aspect of the Self that aggressively stands against inauthentic living and will actively destroy what the ego has falsely taken on as its way of being in the world. On a personal level, the dream suggested to Rosa that the qualities she associated with her mother could be revisioned and revalued in her quest to live her life from a truer base. The aggressiveness, dominance, and uncaring she had loathed in her mother could be used to stand up for herself and against the pull of old attitudes that had never truly served her life and were no longer necessary. In subsequent dreams, the Kali-like woman continued to appear as "helper," instructing Rosa in ways to claim for herself the value she had so often projected to others, and to ruthlessly dispense with the inner and outer critics she had once tried so hard to please. Spurred on by this energy of the relentless Dark Goddess, Rosa finally began to dominate her own life, to claim back what belonged to her and get rid of what did not. In the background was the negative transformative Goddess, lending Her energy to the now Self-serving ego.

Seeing through our personal experience of our mothers to the Goddess dimension brings new meaning and vitality to our lives, as it did for Amy and Rosa. But, even unknown, She appears as the backdrop of the mother–daughter relationship, as in the following poem:

## THREE GENERATIONS

There are three women dining in a cool salmon room
reflecting in a long and deeply scarred table of polished
    wood
once fine untouchable beauty now dull and usable
Ignored are the smudges and splatters of fruit
Blood drops of meat don't matter
They eat with the nonchalance of old friends
The spill of a drink is of no concern to them
and the slip of a knife can be overlooked

The old woman silently reigns over the long scarred
    table
She is ancient as the air that breathed life into
matter and spoke the words "Create us"

Her plate is clean
but for the ceremoniously laid knife and fork upon it
A bowl of ripe and sweating plums sleeps
untouched by her twisted hands.
She is full, and content to have finished her meal before
    them
She waits to leave the table as a common courtesy to
    those who are not done.

The young one sits opposite the old and with her finger
follows a scratch upon the surface of the long scarred
    table.
She travels its length to reach the bowl of sweaty fruit.
The taste and texture suit her
The smooth firm skin slips from her grasp and escapes
    to the
                                        middle of the table
    where it is recaptured, reeled back and slaughtered
Satisfied
all that remains is one pit on its side upon her plate
and the blood of fruit upon her hands.

Sitting halfway between them is another woman staring
at the round damp mark of sweat in the middle of the
    long
                                        scarred table

A witness to the crimes of theft and murder
Nothing is heard or said between them
The old woman will leave soon
The youngest will stay for dessert and the woman in the
    middle
will scrape a dead meal from the plates of a silent feast
gaze into the dining room mirror, and see shrouded in
    pink
                                that there are three women
One is ancient as air
one is young
and one is halfway here and there
and hung from silent threads of yearning to be both.[15]

The poet was unknown to me when I first came across the poem. When I contacted her and asked about the imagery in her poem, she told me that she had never heard of the Goddess and had no knowledge of Her triple form. Consciously, she was writing a poem about her mother, herself, and her three-year-old daughter. Yet the "old woman . . . ancient as the air that breathed life into matter and spoke the words 'Create us' " is a deeply moving vision of the Crone. The depiction of the little girl as thief and murderess is a remarkable recapitulation of the Maiden's secret affinity with the Crone and transformation into Her, which appears in various myths (thus Demeter's child Kore, for example, transforms into the goddess Persephone, "She-who-brings-destruction," after Her abduction to the land of the Dead).[16] Only the Mother is pale in this vision, coming through only as witness to Maiden and Crone. Perhaps the poet had still to discover Her full-bodied splendor, the Mother who is so much more than "halfway here and there," who is a Presence and a magnitude in Herself.

The task of truly coming to terms with our mothers and our experiences of them is twofold. On the one hand, we need to see and forgive their humanness. And perhaps we too must be forgiven the impossible expectations we heap upon their heads. There is an urgent need, a *human* need, for us to come to accept that our mothers are *like* ourselves, just as limited, unsure at times, and the products of their own histories and culture just as we are. To grant our mothers a *personal* self and to grasp that that self does not exist *for* us, that "mother" is only a part of their lives, not the center and not the whole, is to take the first step of differentiating the personal from the transpersonal and to give the personal its proper weight. We may not agree with or even like the women our mothers actually are but, to truly relate to them, we must grant them individuality and their birthright of human limitation.

On the other hand, we need also to see our mothers as carriers of an archetype, a huge image complex that every human being across time and space has had some experience of. Because it is collective and timeless and comes from a very deep layer of the collective psyche, the archetypal Mother appears to us in many of Her ancient trappings; She comes trailing a spiritual history in which we too are included. She is far bigger than our human mothers but comes through them in partial forms. Understanding these partial expressions, these "windows" into the Goddess that our mothers afford us, we can begin to apprehend the whole of Her and name that greater Mother for whom our souls are searching.

The unhealed daughter is searching for her Mother, a Mother whose magnitude fills every corner of her soul. By recognizing that the object of her hunger is much greater than what can possibly be provided by our personal mothers, we can pry the unhealed child loose from her fixation on one human being and teach her to spread out her needs. Becoming open to receiving Mother through more than one source enables a fuller range of healing for her wounds. We must teach the unhealed child to turn toward other women, toward nature, art, meditation, fantasy, and dreams to experience that greater whole. Even to imagine the Great Mother is to create a space for Her, a "home" within us She can once again return to. We must actively cultivate our capacity for image. We must take the unhealed child beyond her insistence that everything be "good" and help her make meaning of what is experienced as "bad"—to honor the mixture of radiance and darkness that the Mother, both human and Goddess, embraces. Being held by this Mother, we may find ourselves able to perceive and receive the healing She brings that extends to our mothers as well, who are also Her needy daughters.

The vision of a contemporary woman encompasses these possibilities. It is a vision for us all. This woman described:

> I had had a dream about conflict between me and my mother. The energy between us was intense. I woke feeling awful. I re-entered the dream through active imagination, feeling the weight of responsibility for my mother that I have always carried, the sense of being overburdened with her emotional needs. In the fantasy, I was cradling her and rocking her but full of despair and resentment. I understood the difficulties between us on an intellectual level, because of her background and my own, but could not accept them emotionally.
>
> We were by the ocean. I was crying as I held her in my arms. Then suddenly, I felt myself no longer on the ground. I was being carried as well. Something was gently rocking me. I looked up and there was a *huge* figure of the Goddess, as big as a mountain. I was on Her lap, still holding my mother. We were sitting out over the water.
>
> My resentment disappeared. I had the feeling of being held and sustained. I realized it wasn't my own strength that I had to depend on.

Ultimately, the Goddess stands behind our personal mother experiences and carries us all.

# 9

# ONE WOMAN'S JOURNEY

I'd like to turn now to a story of a modern woman with whom I worked, whose inner and outer journey reflect some of the problems and resources inherent in working through the mother–daughter relationship today. Trisha was the divorced mother of twin twelve-year-old boys who came to me saying that she was tired of being overweight and that she had problems relating to her sons. At the time she began work with me, both she and her sons had lived with her mother for the past twelve years.

Her father had left the family when she was three; she had few memories of him. She was raised in the company of three women: her mother and two aunts. Her mother had never had any relationships with men after her father.

At first Trisha told me that her mother was like a sister to her: "We go everywhere together," she said. This turned out to be the mother's image of their relationship.

When I asked her what her mother was like as a person, she went blank. I said, trying to help her articulate her sense of her mother, "You know, what's her personality like?" "I don't know," she said. Since she was very artistic, I asked her if she could draw her mother. What emerged was astonishing: She drew a primitive fish-woman, half-fish, half-human (one of the oldest representations of the Goddess), as her mother and drew herself as much smaller, faceless, and attached to her mother from the back (there was a cord that went from back to back between them).

Trisha was unaware of the extent of her attachment to her mother and its connection to her facelessness. What was also striking about the drawing is that neither she nor her mother were *personal.*

Gradually, a more personal picture of her mother emerged. Trisha experienced her as intellectual, verbal, competitive, opinionated, and very concerned about her daughter's mental health. Feelings, especially depression, and fantasy life were especially suspect and worried over. The message Trisha repeatedly got was that she couldn't do anything on her own, a powerful message from her binding mother.

When I first met the mother, she struck me as self-righteous. Also striking was that in Trisha's presence she often either spoke for her or about her as if Trisha weren't there. In her mother's presence, Trisha was silent and withdrawn.

In the beginning of our work, Trisha was a timid, self-effacing woman and had almost no sense of a personal self or self-worth. She had great difficulty expressing feelings and was barely verbal. At the same time, she had tremendous artistic gifts and a very rich inner life. She drew and painted the way some people dream; it was not unusual for her to bring me four paintings a session. Her paintings were almost all of archetypal imagery, religious and mythological visions. She had no personal connection to her work at this time and was often frightened by the images that came through her. She was what Toni Wolff has described as a "medial woman,"[1] a visionary through whom archetypal images express themselves. She herself, however, had no relation to these images. In addition, her artistic expression was constricted; she couldn't use color, for example, when she first came to me because colors meant feelings to her, and feelings were too frightening. Her mother had wanted to be an artist herself but didn't have the skills; she became a columnist for a local newspaper instead. When Trisha asked her mother if she, Trisha, could be an artist, her mother said no, she wasn't good enough.

In the second session, Trisha brought me a series of twenty-eight drawings. She had no idea what they meant. In retrospect, they were like an initial dream, setting the stage for the entire analytic process. They depicted the journey of a young woman leaving a sterile castle with only women in it. After many encounters and obstacles, she comes to the Mother's City, where she is initiated into womanhood through blood mysteries and dance. Then she journeys to the Father's City, where she meets the man who becomes her husband. They have a son but eventually both father and son die and she becomes the ruler, fully female but with a powerful male spirit as her guide. Although she had no sense of personal connection to this, the drawing series was a complete description of what took place in the course of analysis.

At first, there was little differentiation from her mother. She shared everything with her, including her dreams, but sometimes she felt that she wanted a little space from her. She was surprised when I wouldn't agree to work with her mother, too. I began to encourage her to think about how *she* felt and what *she* wanted in everyday situations.

She had little relationship to her sons; her mother was raising them, and Trisha felt more like their sister than their mother. She feared their maleness and felt helpless to deal with their problems. This we worked on concretely, going through ordinary issues such as how to become more involved with their school situations.

Our focus at first was essentially practical; I was trying to help her begin to get some personal grounding in the world. This was very important because her mother had convinced her that she couldn't handle practical things. She felt she could never handle money, pay bills, or keep house. All of these were her mother's domain. Instead of being matrophobic, Trisha took on her mother's image of her, merged with it, and was convinced that she was as inadequate as her mother said she was.

We focused a lot on sexuality and her body as well, which carried her sense of not being worth much and her negative feelings about being a woman. She had had strong sexual feelings since childhood; her mother had seen her as "oversexed" at eight or nine years of age because she had been found engaged in sex play with other children and because she became attached to men who visited the house to do repairs. She felt her sexual feelings to be strongly taboo and had gained weight at the age of ten to get away from them. She hated her body, felt it was shit or rot, that it was disgusting. Interestingly, she overate sweets; her mother was a diabetic and thin. Eating what the mother could not and being fat were her only ways of being separate from her mother. Talking about her sexual feelings and her body was releasing for Trisha. She began to feel a re-awakening, as if she were re-experiencing puberty. I was already beginning to be something of a countermother for her, someone she could use to help differentiate herself from her mother.

She wove an image around me that revisioned what she found unacceptable about herself. She drew a woman with magical powers, a red cloth of menstrual blood across her lap. She said this woman initiated girls into womanhood and associated her with me. The initiate, who she felt was herself, was nude with emphasized erogenous zones (much like some of the most ancient pictures of the Goddess).[2]

She already had a sense of the numinous Feminine with powers different from her mother's; now she struggled to define a different sense of her body. She wrote:

> I suddenly have the strong feeling that it is all *right* to be fat. Since I wouldn't look at the shadow side of Catholicism, it overtook me physically wherever I went. So now I see the demon of hunger as an honest peasant god, *real* and not about to let me go or I would leave the female religion behind. But if I could turn to him as a friend—as the real inductor into this femaleness and love him and the female body I carry, that makes it right to be fat. In this I find myself fighting with Jung, with his statement that a man who actually liked fat women was not out of the matriarchal phase. It has felt to me as though this would also apply to a woman who was fat—

> but now I feel that the statement may be true but fat is coming back—as female is coming back. I feel [Jung's] statement to be derogatory and it should not be. It is *good* to be in the matriarchal orientation because this *has* to come to the surface. The ugly stuff must come to the surface and be recognized as not evil. Fat is ugly and wrong today because it is *female*, not because it's wrong.

In one session she spoke of how she had no sense of uniqueness except through her painting. I asked her to consider what else might make her unique and she answered, "My fat; my fat means I won't get lost in a crowd and no one can mistake me for a boy."

Eight months after we began working, she took the first big step of separating from her mother; she moved into the basement of their shared home and began for the first time to have a sense of a space of her own. She insisted on splitting money and separating bills in spite of her mother's resistance to this.

She was frightened and unsure of her own stance but a sense of separateness was blooming. She told me, for example, that she had a chair that her mother hated. Trisha felt that she couldn't have what she called "bad taste" (which meant what her mother didn't like)—and then she hesitated and said *she* liked the chair and had her *own* taste.

She began to develop shared interests with her sons, separate from her mother's involvement with them. And she also began to make female friends.

She was aware now of her attachment to her mother and the merging she had to struggle against. She wrote:

> Every effort I have made had a built-in failure. I think I fear failure enough so that I see to it that it is going to happen so it can't surprise me. And I think it's due to the fact that my mother feels you *cannot* succeed at art and also that she told me I could not be an artist. I apparently proved her wrong there; I can draw—but what to do to make a living at it or at any work I find even bearable is beyond me.

> It's the same thing with marriage. I picked a marriage with built-in failure so I couldn't be surprised by failure. After all, *hers* failed and she was greater than I, so mine couldn't succeed. I *cannot* be more successful than she. Apparently that is a law I run headlong into. The unconscious succeeded in getting around that in art.
>
> She is not good in math—so I am not good at math. She would not be good in a business so I would not be good in business. She was not good in science so I cannot, by nature, be good in science.
>
> But the two areas she felt very poor in—imagination and art—I succeeded in. Yet they were both areas she was working in, trying her own wings. So maybe that gave me permission. . . .
>
> Still the question remains—how do I find out what I'm *good* at? I can work (under protest), I can drive (my mother can't), I can paint and carve and model clay.

Later, anger and criticism of her mother began to surface along with a more positive evaluation of herself. She wrote:

> I'm beginning also to feel the lack of trust (by my mother). I am not trusted to be a good housekeeper, a good mother, to know how to handle money. I am the student, the introvert, and as such I am too one-sided, my mother says, to do these things. This is the message I have been living with. Yet I can enjoy keeping a house and I can be a good mother even when I'm screaming at the children. Now I do very little screaming or even scolding and *she* screams at them.
>
> I feel perfectly competent with money and also did handle it when I was married. Yet *she* distrusts me with money while she is prone to paying bills weeks ahead of time and leaving us with *no* food money. Last time we paid the bills, she panicked and said as she made out the last one, that we didn't have the money. Yet when I asked what the balance was, it turned out we would have over a hundred left and still have a penny bank of $80. Yet I can't handle money and she can. I think the base of that might be that I can and will spend on personal

> things like rings when there is money and she doesn't, but that's *her* problem.

Soon after this, she began to fear her mother's invading her. She was now painting prolifically and in color, and here too she made a courageous declaration of self:

> I did the end of my painting [she wrote], the one of Mother Earth Dreaming the Crucifixion. I started painting early in the day at [my friend's house], then found myself getting dizzy and nauseous, even feeling faint. I was definitely connecting it to the painting which I now knew I would sign [she had never signed a painting before] as though finally committing myself to something—here was my statement and my grounding, where I stood in the middle of my painting and from that standpoint looked out at the world. As though also it was a break with my mother, a declaration that this was my field and that I was now different from her.
>
> It felt like I was standing alone on a mountaintop and I had stepped upward higher than my mother had and therefore it was very dangerous—unsteady and easy to fall from—because it was beyond my mother. Her support couldn't be there. I was finally on ground she had *not* tread.

Finally, nearly a year after we started working, she moved into her own apartment with her sons. She felt disoriented by this but also exhilarated. Right after she moved, she dreamed of her mother's death. This terrified her; she couldn't go to work because of her fear. She wanted badly to stay separate but had to go over to her mother's house and make sure she was all right.

In my experience, this is a common, deep, underlying theme in mother–daughter separation for some women, especially when there has been a binding mother with whom the daughter has been merged. The belief is: If I take on my own life, my mother will die. Sometimes this reflects some of the mother's investment in the daughter but, in my experience, it has more to do with the daughter's loss of that mother and of the orientation that being connected to her mother gave her. Letting go means giving up what's familiar, and what's familiar is safe because it's known. Even if the familiar is horrible and life killing, this is true. If the mother is relinquished, the mother's daughter must find out who she is outside of the adaptation she made to the mother. If the hold of the mother is broken, it *is* a death and makes way for the daughter's rebirth.

This is movingly illustrated in Trisha's writings after she moved into her own apartment:

> [I've] been trying to think what it means or feels like to be *alone* in my new place. Closest I can come to describing it is that it's as though I am and have been frozen. And slowly, *very* slowly, as I sit time after time, being alone, I think I can feel the thawing setting in. I don't know what my insides are because they have been frozen for years.
>
> I almost feel that left on my own, with no pull from the outside world or from the collective unconscious, I might have no energy at all and feel like I'm in the void that's me—and it has to be a void because it's frozen and it can't have any energy now because it's never been used.

Later, during the same period, she wrote:

> I find that I still feel uptight after getting home. Like I'm thawing *into* my apartment. Like it's still so new that I don't know what to do with it. Like getting used to a new baby.

Two months later, she was finding her own way. She wrote:

> I looked at the door Billy, Matt [her sons], and I retrieved from the garbage and saw it as a table and it suddenly dawned on me that I had been *terrified* of being by myself—on my own—and I now *was* and that I was able to cope with it. Even though it's a painful process to cope with figuring out where thousands of things *go*. I'm now, for the first time, getting a feel for the apartment

> in the sense of what to do with the *things*. As though with the door and the arrival of my regular table, the pieces are all *here* and now they are beginning to fall into place.

Her sense of her body and herself as a woman were also changing. She realized that some of her negative feelings about her body stemmed from never having been touched as a child; she felt her mother had never loved her physically.

I was a strong model for her at this time of what had been taboo and what she now wanted to claim. Although I acknowledged that I too had problems with weight, she saw me as carrying my weight well and having prettier clothes than she. I encouraged her to use her envy to let herself know and have what she wanted (she had up to this point always worn shapeless, ragged clothes). Now she experimented with new, more attractive clothes and eventually found a style all her own.

She painted me as very sexual, wearing bright colors. She saw me as "half in consciousness and half in the unconscious, but you don't lose yourself in the unconscious." I was a model of her budding ego which was beginning not only to enable her to connect more adequately to the outer world but also to develop some grounding in relationship to her powerful inner life.

I encouraged her to paint her feelings about her body. She painted her body covered with hair, connected it with Sleeping Beauty and Beauty and the Beast, "but the beast is me," she said. She felt that her body was struggling to get out.

The beginning of her separation from me came about in a most profound way. She was somewhat familiar with the imagery of the Goddess and the Old Religion because at one point I'd given her Merlin Stone's *When God Was a Woman* to read. Periodically, the Goddess popped up in one of her paintings in various forms but she did not have a strong personal connection with these images. Other imagery was more central and more important to her.

About two years after we'd begun our work, she came in

one session very shaken, saying she had had a powerful vision of the Great Mother. It was too powerful to describe in words but two things had come out of it; she realized that the Great Mother was *all* and was sexual. She was profoundly affected by this. She told me that she now realized that to touch her body was to touch the Goddess and that all women were a piece of the Goddess's body. Having grown an ego, she was now in touch with a feminine Self, a profound and transpersonal vision of wholeness.

Two months later, she felt compelled to build a shrine for the Goddess. She put it in her closet. In the session that followed her building of the shrine, she told me that she felt very frightened. Part of it was that she felt she had left the church and was worshiping a pagan goddess, but part of it seemed connected with the shrine itself.

I asked if she could image the threat. At first she thought of a housekeeper her mother had employed when she was three years old; she had felt that this woman hated her. Then she thought of an aunt who had been a nurse and had treated her when she had had hepatitis; she pictured her aunt now with a huge hypodermic needle. Finally, the figure became a *huge* housekeeper. When I asked her to image it further, the figure became very threatening. I told Trisha to ask this figure what it wanted.

The answer was, "I want you." "What does she want with you?" I asked, entering this active imagination. Trisha's answer was: "To eat me up." Why?" I asked. "So that she can be free; she is attached to me. I am her food; then she will have weight." Fearfully, Trisha began to talk about sacrifice. "Can anything be substituted?" I asked. "Yes," the figure of the Housekeeper said, "a soul stone." Now, recently, Trisha had found a stone that she had felt carried a great sense of power; she had named it her soul stone. Hearing the Housekeeper's answer, Trisha wondered whether she wouldn't lose her own soul then. I encouraged her to ask if something else could be found, to tell the Housekeeper that that stone was Trisha's and couldn't be given. The answer was yes, Trisha could go down to the river and find a white speckled stone; that would do.

Suddenly Trisha realized that what this woman, this goddess, wanted was a place in the shrine; she didn't want to be left out. I thought of the thirteenth fairy in Sleeping Beauty who curses the child because she's left out of the celebrations of her birth. She represents whatever aspect of the Feminine has been devalued, shut out, prevented from bestowing its blessing on life and so it returns in twisted, threatening form. In Trisha this devalued aspect appeared in her difficulty with doing housework which was in part a reaction to her mother's pronouncement that she was inferior in this area and couldn't manage it. The threatening Housekeeper figure that appeared in her fantasy experience demanded that this, too, be included in her honoring of the Goddess, that this issue in her life be referred to a higher authority than her devaluing mother. What was interesting was that when Trisha finished her shrine, including now a stone for the Housekeeper, she could do a lot of housework herself without her usual anxiety or sense of inferiority about it.

She began actively to worship the Goddess. She said, "I feel like I'm the earth and my axis is changing." In this same period, she dreamed of a baby who was cured of a hereditary disease.

The Housekeeper's daughter began to appear to her in visions. On a personal level, Trisha connected this figure to the actual daughter of the housekeeper her mother had employed, a girl who had turned against her nasty mother. Now the rebellious one was elevated to a holy figure and Trisha felt that if something was too small to take to the Goddess, she could take it to the daughter first.

She spoke of feeling sent out from the shrine into her daily life: into housework, keeping herself on a diet, into her job. She now had a more solid inner grounding for her ego, a matrix for her feminine self.

Many things began to change. Her bond with her sons deepened and she was able to support their newly adolescent needs for autonomy. She began to relate to a man after many years of not relating to men; this was very difficult and brought up many issues around her absent father. At the same time, her mother—who had really taken on her own issues and separation needs as a result of her own therapy—fell in love and got married, at the age of seventy.

This was electrifying for Trisha, especially because her stepfather began to fill in a father image for her—although the two of them had many difficulties and clashes of personality. In her inner life, Trisha now began to connect with male god images and added a male god to figures on her altar to the Goddess. Then, gradually, she built a separate shrine for God the Father.

At this point, she took off into previously forbidden territory. She began to have powerful experiences of inner male figures who strengthened her belief in herself as an artist and powerfully affected her sense of herself and her art. She painted even more than before and began to write mythic stories for the figures she was painting. Her writing became as prolific as her painting, which was also interesting because writing had previously been only her mother's territory. At one point she wasn't sure I would understand her anymore. Her inner male guide said that was because I was in the South in the realm of the Goddess and she was in the North. Both were valid, he said; we were just in different places.

The end of the story is full and remarkable. Trisha and her mother eventually became friends, mutually supportive, aware of their differences, fully separate. I knew the mother quite well at this point; what was striking was how different she and Trisha were. The mother was very practical and down to earth, with a rich good humor. Her daughter was much more inner, more idiosyncratic and exotic. Trisha's mother now accepted their differences and had done her own separating.

Trisha made radical changes. She quit the boring job she had worked at and devoted full time to her art. She lived communally for a while with her parents until one of her inner guides told her to move to Mexico. Her stepfather was particularly affected by this. A very conservative, military man, he was somehow touched deeply and said that he, too, wanted to follow a dream. Her mother, too, was affected. Remarkably, they all decided to take instruction from Trisha's inner guide and move to Mexico.

At this point, *I* became the practical, conservative mother; I worried constantly. How would she live? How would they have a roof over their heads? etc. At one point I was quite dubious and discouraging but by this time Trisha had such a strong sense of her own center that she took me on and said she was going anyway.

The move to Mexico was an important experience for all of them. In time, her stepfather returned and was followed by her mother. Trisha remained and wrote me of deeper involvements with men and with what she felt as the previously alien Father world. She came back pregnant and decided to have the baby even though she was no longer connected to the father. The last time I spoke with Trisha, she had just begun painting again. She was nursing the baby who was being cared for not only by her but by an extended group of family and friends. She said she was very happy.

Trisha's life is a more precarious one than some of us could live, but it is fully hers and individual now. I learned a great deal from her about creativity, introverted values, and following one's own way. It moves me to remember and share her story, and I am grateful to her for allowing me to do so.

We see in the story of Trisha a full picture of mother–daughter separation and relationship, which includes the following:

1. Separation and differentiation from the personal mother
2. Reclaiming and rebirthing of the child that had not been adequately facilitated into her own growth
3. The helpfulness of another woman as counter-mother
4. The constellation of the archetype as an inner

resource and the willingness of the ego to learn from it and serve it

5. And, finally, in Trisha's case, a fine reconnecting with her personal mother in a way that allowed for the fullness and differences of both.

# CONCLUSION

The process of making meaning for our lives goes on, consciously and unconsciously. As in the Old Religion, where Life and Death, positive and negative, were continually recycling, each giving rise to the other, so in our psyches the images through which we see cycle and change. This is true of the inner mother, the image through which we remember or see our outer mothers. Long-forgotten memories, suddenly welling up into consciousness, may shift our image of her. New information about her life, or new psychological perspectives in our own that we are introduced to as we go along, recreate the image. We think we know who our mothers are, but our images shift and transform. We can see this easily if we look across the space of our entire lives and recall the images we saw her through at different ages. Even if our mothers are dead, this shifting can happen and bring healing in its wake. And this is the wonder of the psyche and the base of many a spiritual experience: Images alone, psychic experience alone, can heal even the vacancies and wounds of what was literally experienced once but is no longer accessible on a literal level.

I remember an experience of this that unfolded in a workshop I did years ago. We were talking about body and touch in the mother–daughter relationship and I had taken the group into a guided fantasy about their mothers and their bodies. After leading the group through a progressive relaxation exercise, I asked each woman to picture herself in a setting she particularly loved and to feel the goodness of her body, to feel herself truly *in* her body and loving it. Then I asked her to imagine her mother coming into the scene and to let the fantasy go on open ended. This was a powerful exercise for many of the women in the workshop but one woman especially emerged from it looking radiant. I asked if she could share her experience with the group and she told the following story: She had imaged herself on the farm she'd grown up on, by the stream where she loved to play. She was standing there naked, feeling deeply at home, when her mother appeared, also naked. They dove into the stream together and swam side by side. Then they transformed into fish, swimming and playing in the water. In reality, she went on to tell us, she had never even seen her mother's body and there had been little physical bonding between them. And now her mother had been dead for many years. Yet something *happened* in her during the fantasy. It was as if it had really taken place; something that had been so missing in her relationship with her mother had been touched and healed. She could feel the shift inside her. Her face was filled with tenderness and wonder as she spoke.

Writing this book, I have had a similar experience, completely unexpected and deeply moving to me. It came in a dream, interweaving past and present, personal and transpersonal in a new and meaningful way. It was several weeks into the writing of this book when I had this dream. I had been trying unsuccessfully to write the positive memories of my bond with my grandmother that introduce the second chapter. Every time I would be overwhelmed with sadness and have to stop. Then I dreamed: I was with my grandmother in the backyard of my childhood home. The pignut tree that had stood in the yard in my childhood was now the Apple Tree that stands in my backyard today. It was blossoming and I thought of cutting some of the branches to put in a vase.

The backyard *was* my grandmother's; it contained the largest part of her garden and was probably where she and I spent the most time together, aside from the kitchen. The pignut tree was a huge, old tree that dominated the yard; I liked to gather its nuts and play with them. It has also a current connection for me. Last year I discovered another pignut tree—the first I have seen since my childhood—in the backyard of a woman who has taught me deeply what it is like to be positively mothered. When I was visiting her, I found one of the nuts that had fallen from the tree. It was stripped bare of its hull and exquisitely beautiful, its fullness coming to a miniscule point. I had thought of it then as a tiny nature breast and had carried it around for weeks.

The Apple Tree has profound meaning for me. It has carried one of my deepest and fullest experiences of the positive transformative Goddess. When I first moved, many years ago, to the house I live in now, I had an eerie experience in my backyard. I felt a Presence in the apple tree that grew there; there was something *there* within and beyond the tree itself. At the time I didn't know that apples and apple trees had been sacred to the Goddess. Nor had I ever had this kind of experience before, though I have since experienced it, when I once unknowingly drove into sacred Indian ground upstate and felt, before I knew where I was, a powerful sense of Presence. But with the apple tree, I was quite unnerved. Slowly, I began to tune to this Presence and become more open to it. I sensed from the start that it was Feminine and realized I was being encountered by some powerful aspect of the Goddess. For several years, this Being-in-the-Tree became a kind of spirit guide to me, with whom I had many inner dialogues. Most often, She functioned as Teacher and compassionate Companion, instructing me deeply about Herself, about Life and Death, about myself in the present and the past. Sometimes She spoke to me about my grandmother. At times, Her instruction was more than I felt ready for, Her lessons more than I could bear, yet always She taught with benevolence and I grew to trust this spirit profoundly. She is mostly silent now, and there are other aspects of the Goddess that are more prominent in my current life. Yet the spirit of the Apple Tree remains with me, like a first positive mothering. . . .

The dream plants Her in my childhood. I scarcely have words to convey what that means to me. It changes my perception of the past. It means She was there in the sweetness between my grandmother and me. It means She was there for my grandmother, in "her" space as well as mine, and that She dominated a space that was also "ours." It means there is something more in the present than the wrenching sadness I often feel when I think about my grandmother. She is there, too, bigger than my sadness, bigger than the events that seemed to overtake my grandmother and me. It means that something in the present, something huge in its meaning and benevolence, has been transported to my past and stands there as well, just as the pignut tree now stands in the yard of the woman who has been one of the "good mothers" I have known in adulthood. Past and present interweave, interflow. To me, this bespeaks a continuity that I have rarely been aware of in my life and exemplifies an essential, ongoing creativeness in both the Goddess and myself. Seen as a vision of Her, it reminds me of one of my favorite poems about Her by a woman who calls the Goddess "She Who":

> She Who continues.
> She Who has a being
> named She Who is a being
> named She Who carries her own name.
> She Who turns things over.
> She Who marks her own way, gathering.
> She Who makes her own difference.
> She Who differs, gathering her own events.
> She Who gathers, gaining
> She Who carries her own ways,
> gathering She Who waits,
> bearing She Who cares for her
> own name, carrying She Who
> bears, carrying She Who cares
> for She Who gathers her own ways,
> carrying
> the names of She Who gather and gain,
> singing: I am the woman, the woman
> the woman—I am the first person
> and the first person is She Who is the first person to
> She Who is the first person to no other. There is no
> other first person.

She Who floods like a river and
like a river continues
She Who continues[1]

The process goes on. In my life and yours, She continues.

# NOTES

## INTRODUCTION

1. Adrienne Rich, *Of Woman Born* (New York: W. W. Norton, 1976), pp. 222–224.

## CHAPTER 1. THREE PERSPECTIVES

1. See Chapters 3–8 in Dorothy Dinnerstein, *The Mermaid and the Minotaur* (New York: Harper and Row, 1976), for further discussion of the consequences of patriarchal child-rearing arrangements. Dinnerstein focuses on the antagonisms toward women that are engendered by female-dominated child care, which "include an assumption that [the mother] exists as a natural resource, as an asset to be owned and harnessed, harvested and mined, with no fellow-feeling for depletion and no responsibility for her conservation or replenishment" (p. 36). Similarly, Marge Piercy expresses the ill fit of such assumptions in her powerful poem "Magic Mama" in her book *My Mother's Body* (New York: Alfred A. Knopf, 1985), pp. 78–79.
2. See Adrienne Rich, *Of Woman Born,* for an exemplary discussion of this differentiation between motherhood as personal experience and as societal institution.
3. Nancy Chodorow has written a scholarly analysis of the ways women replicate and pass on mothering patterns from generation to generation in unconscious service of society's values and views of women in her classic, *The Reproduction of Mothering* (Berkeley and Los Angeles: University of California Press, 1978).
4. Rich, *Of Woman Born,* p. 251. See also Nancy Friday's story of her Aunt Kate in her book, *My Mother, My Self* (New York: Delacorte Press, 1977), pp. 192–196.
5. After the manuscript for *In Her Image* was already completed, I came across an extremely well-balanced and helpful consideration of the role of anger in the healing of survivors of childhood abuse in Ellen Bass and Laura Davis's book, *The Courage to Heal: A Guide for Women Survivors*

*of Child Sexual Abuse* (New York: Harper and Row, 1988), the section entitled "Anger—The Backbone of Healing," pp. 122–132. In the present context, see especially "Working through Mother Blame" on p. 125, which aims at helping women differentiate between displacing anger at an abusive father onto their mothers and legitimate, proportional anger at mothers who were abusive themselves or failed to protect their daughters from an abusive other.

6. See, for example, Gloria Steinem's deeply moving story of her mother, "Ruth's Song (Because She Could Not Sing It)" in her book, *Outrageous Acts and Everyday Rebellions* (New York: Holt, Rhinehart, and Winston, 1983), pp. 129–146. Steinem conveys deep compassion and sensitivity toward her mother, who was frequently mentally ill, and exposes the personal and social/institutional factors that loomed large in her mother's experience. Her tale is a harrowing one of struggling to survive both emotionally and literally from the age of ten on while acting as her mother's primary caretaker. Yet there is curiously little feeling for the child in herself who received so very little care, or for her own deprivation and hunger for nurturing. Instead she writes of being obsessed now "with the things I could have done for my mother while she was alive or the things I should have said" (p. 144). Deftly and with great sensitivity, Steinem articulates a feminist view of her mother's plight but deflects a more personal focus on herself as her mother's daughter.

## CHAPTER 2. POSITIVE BONDS

1. Anne Sexton, *The Complete Poems* (Boston: Houghton Mifflin, 1981), pp. 464–465.
2. Quoted in Karen Payne (ed.), *Between Ourselves: Letters between Mothers and Daughters* (Boston: Houghton Mifflin, 1983), p. 143.
3. Payne, *Between Ourselves,* pp. 140–142.
4. Friday, *My Mother, My Self,* pp. 197–198; Judith Arcana, *Our Mothers' Daughters* (Berkeley: Shameless Hussy Press, 1979), pp. 165–166.
5. Tillie Olsen's short story, "I Stand Here Ironing" in her book *Tell Me a Riddle* (New York: Dell Publishing, 1960), pp. 1–12, vividly depicts the disruption of a basically loving mother–daughter bond due to such factors as the pressures

of single-parenting, inadequate child-care resources, the stress of several children to care for, and the social influence of war and economic depression.

6. See Judith Arcana, Chapter 5, "Fathers: The Men in Our Lives" in *Our Mothers' Daughters,* pp. 119–145 for further discussion of the impact of the father–daughter relationship on the mother–daughter bond.
7. Adrienne Rich describes her early sense of having been sacrificed to her father's educational programs by her mother, who was held responsible for carrying out his theories of "enlightened, unorthodox child-rearing," pp. 222–223, *Of Woman Born.*

## CHAPTER 3. THE BINDING OR BANISHING MOTHER

1. Payne, *Between Ourselves,* p. 6.
2. See Jane Flax's paper, "The Conflict between Nurturance and Autonomy in Mother–Daughter Relationships and within Feminism" in *Feminist Studies,* Vol. 4, No. 2, June 1978, pp. 171–189, for a Freudian-oriented discussion of why many mothers and daughters have difficulty negotiating a relationship that allows both a nurturant bond between them and support for separateness and independence.
3. Anne Sexton, *The Complete Poems,* pp. 41–42.
4. Signe Hammer, *Daughters and Mothers, Mothers and Daughters,* NY: The New American Library, Inc., 1975, p. 109.
5. Hammer, *Daughters and Mothers,* p. 111.
6. See the letters between Jessica and her mother in Payne, *Between Ourselves,* pp. 25–31, for an example of the threat to the mother when a daughter chooses a life-style other than traditional marriage.

## CHAPTER 4. TOUCH IN THE MOTHER–DAUGHTER RELATIONSHIP

1. See Adrienne Rich's discussion of maternal violence in *Of Woman Born,* Chapter X, pp. 256–280.
2. See sections on "mother–daughter incest" in Bass and Davis's *The Courage to Heal,* pp. 96–97 and pp. 387–393.
3. See Sylvia Perera's comments on "controlled therapeutic regression" in her *Descent to the Goddess* (Toronto: Inner City Books, 1981), pp. 56–58.

4. Arcana, *Our Mothers' Daughters,* pp. 71–87; *c.f.* Lucy Rose Fischer's view that "The daughter's physical development has a dual and contradictory meaning for the mother-daughter relationship: It represents both their bond as females and the greatest barrier between them—their heterosexuality" (p. 39), Lucy Rose Fischer, *Linked Lives: Adult Daughters and Their Mothers,* (New York: Harper and Row, 1986).

## CHAPTER 5. MATROPHOBIA AND ITS TRANSFORMATION

1. Maxine Kumin in Lyn Lifshin (ed.), *Tangled Vines: A Collection of Mother and Daughter Poems* (Boston: Beacon Press, 1978), p. 85.
2. Rich, *Of Woman Born,* p. 235.
3. Carl Jung, "Psychological Aspects of the Mother Archetype" in his *Collected Works,* Vol. 9(*i*), NY: Bollingen Foundation, 1959, pp. 90–91. Although many feminists do not like his views of women and the archetypal Feminine, Jung very early on understood the destructive effects of projections upon women and even pleaded that the weight of the archetypal Mother in the form of impossible expectations be taken off the human woman (p. 92).
4. In extreme cases, this may even take the form of deciding not to become a mother out of fear of replicating the maternal pattern (this is especially common, in my experience, among women who were abused in childhood by their mothers and fear becoming abusive themselves).
5. Judith Anderson, "Mother" in Greater Lansing Spinsters' Guild, *The Greengathering Feast* (songs) (East Lansing, Mich.: Tea Rose Press, 1981), p. 41.

## CHAPTER 6. THE UNHEALED CHILD: PARTIAL SOLUTIONS AND HEALING POSSIBILITIES

1. Rich observes, "Whatever our rational forgiveness, whatever the individual mother's love and strengths, the child in us, the small female who grew up in a male-controlled world, still feels, at moments, wildly unmothered" (p. 225), *Of Woman Born.*
2. See Nancy Friday, *My Mother, My Self,* pp. 240–241, also

Chapter 11, "Marriage: The Return to Symbiosis," pp. 337–377; *c.f.* Rich, *Of Woman Born*, pp. 242–243.

3. Rich, *Of Woman Born*, pp. 224–225.

## CHAPTER 7. LIFESOURCE: INTRODUCTION TO THE GREAT MOTHER

1. June Rachuy Brindel, *Ariadne* (New York: St. Martin's Press, 1980), pp. 3–4.
2. Robert Graves, "Introduction" to his book, *The Greek Myths*, Vol. 1 (Middlesex, England: Penguin Books, 1955), pp. 13*ff.* Also see Merlin Stone, *When God Was a Woman* (New York and London: Harcourt Brace Jovanovich, 1976), and Marija Gimbutas, *The Goddesses and Gods of Old Europe: Myths and Cult Images* (Berkeley and Los Angeles: University of California Press, 1982), for the history of the Goddess religion.
3. An essay on the persecution of women as witches that I particularly like is in Starhawk's book, *Dreaming the Dark* (Boston: Beacon Press, 1982), Appendix A, "The Burning Times: Notes on a Crucial Period in History," pp. 183–219.
4. See, for example, the chapter on St. Brigid, in James Preston's *Mother Worship* (Chapel Hill: University of North Carolina Press, 1982), pp. 75–94.
5. See Marina Warner, *Alone of All Her Sex: The Myth and Cult of the Virgin Mary* (New York: Alfred A. Knopf, 1976), for a thorough investigation from a feminist perspective of the imagery, legends, and meanings associated with Mary, including some of her connections with ancient visions of the Goddess.
6. There are many books on women's spirituality that have sprung up in the last decade. Two of the most broadly representative are the collections of essays in Carol Christ and Judith Plaskow (eds.), *Womanspirit Rising* (San Francisco: Harper and Row, 1979), and Charlene Spretnak (ed.), *The Politics of Women's Spirituality* (Garden City, N.Y.: Anchor Press, 1982).
7. See, for example, Sylvia Perera's work on the relevance of the Sumerian goddess Inanna to modern women, in her *Descent to the Goddess*. Interestingly, Carl Jung, writing about the mother Goddess back in 1954, claimed, "The concept [of the Great Mother] itself is of no immediate

concern to psychology because the image of a Great Mother in this form is rarely encountered in [clinical] practice and then only under very special conditions" (*Collected Works*, "Psychological Aspects of the Mother Archetype," p. 75). This is no longer true: The emergence of goddess images in contemporary dreams, fantasy, and artistic productions, as well as the ever-increasing written material on Her religion, ancient and modern, reflect perhaps a shift in the collective unconscious toward making this ancient imagery revisible to the modern man and woman.

8. Carol Christ, "Why Women Need the Goddess" in Christ and Plaskow, *Womanspirit Rising*, pp. 273–287.
9. For a provocative study of the symbolic meaning of menstruation, see Penelope Shuttle and Peter Redgrove's book, *The Wise Wound: Eve's Curse and Everywoman* (New York: Richard Marek Publishers, 1978).
10. See entry under "Menstrual Blood" in Barbara Walker's tome, *The Women's Encyclopedia of Myths and Secrets* (San Francisco: Harper and Row, 1983), pp. 635–645. Walker writes, "Indians of South America said all mankind was made of 'moon blood' in the beginning. The same idea prevailed in ancient Mesopotamia, where the Great Goddess Ninhursag made mankind out of clay and infused it with her 'blood of life.' Under her alternate names of Mammetun or Aruru the Great, the Potter, she taught women to form clay dolls and smear them with menstrual blood as a conception charm, a piece of magic that underlay the name of Adam, from the feminine adamah, meaning 'bloody clay,' though scholars more delicately translate it 'red earth.' The Bible's story of Adam was lifted from an older female-oriented creation myth recounting the creation of man from clay and moon blood" (p. 635).
11. See Barbara Walker's discussion of the wisdom attributed to postmenopausal women in ancient times in her book, *The Crone* (San Francisco: Harper and Row, 1985), especially Chapter 3, "The Wise Crone," pp. 43–68.
12. Gimbutas, *Goddesses and Gods of Old Europe*, p. 112.
13. Stone, *When God Was a Woman*, pp. 154–155.
14. In Diane Wolkstein and Samuel Noah Kramer, *Inanna, Queen of Heaven and Earth* (New York: Harper and Row, 1983), p. 12.
15. Wolkstein and Kramer, *Inanna, Queen of Heaven and Earth*, pp. 36–37.

16. Wolkstein and Kramer, *Inanna*, p. 37.
17. Michael Dames, *The Silbury Treasure* (London: Thames and Hudson, 1976), pp. 94–95. See Jorgen Andersen, *The Witch in the Wall* (Copenhagen: Rosenkilde and Bagger, 1977) for a more thorough discussion of these fascinating figures.
18. See the tale of Erysichthon who was condemned to perpetual hunger by the grain goddess Ceres for cutting down an oak in Her sacred grove, in Ovid's *Metamorphoses* (Middlesex, England: Penguin Books, 1955), pp. 198–202.
19. Quoted in Erich Neumann, *The Great Mother* (New York: Bollingen Foundation, 1955), p. 85.
20. See Sylvia Perera's discussion of the goddess Inanna's Underworld sister Ereshkigal, in Perera, *Descent to the Goddess*, Chapters 2–4, pp. 16–49.
21. Walker, *The Crone*, p. 29.
22. The meaning and value of the fairy-tale witch from a Jungian perspective are discussed in Ann Ulanov's paper, "The Witch Archetype," *Quadrant* (Journal of the C. G. Jung Foundation, New York), Vol. 10, No. 1, Summer 1977, pp. 5–22.
23. *New Larousse Encyclopedia of Mythology* (Middlesex, England: Hamlyn Publishing Group, 1959), p. 36.
24. See the section on Kali in David Kinsley's book, *The Sword and the Flute: Kali and Krsna* (Berkeley and Los Angeles: University of California Press, 1975), pp. 81–159.
25. Swami Nikhilananda, *The Gospel of Sri Ramakrishna* (New York: Ramakrishna-Vivekananda Center, 1952), p. 9.
26. Charles Boer (transl.), *The Homeric Hymns* (Chicago: Swallow Press, 1970), pp. 91–135. For an alternative and sometimes more evocative translation, see Chapter 8, "The Homeric Hymn to Demeter" in Paul Friederich, *The Meaning of Aphrodite* (Chicago and London: University of Chicago Press, 1978), pp. 163–180.
27. Graves, *The Greek Myths*, Vol. 1, p. 93, n. 3.
28. I am picking up on Adrienne Rich's idea of "homesickness" in her poem, "Transcendental Etude" in *Dream of a Common Language*, pp. 75*ff*.
29. Starhawk's *Dreaming the Dark* particularly explicates the vision of the Goddess as immanent. See her explanation of this term on pp. 9–14.

30. Rich, *Of Woman Born*, p. 42, pp. 283–286.
31. See Carol Baumann's paper, "Psychological Experiences Connected with Childbirth," *Studien zur analytischen Psychologie C. G. Jungs*, Vol. 1 (Zurich: Rascher Verlag, 1955), pp. 336–370.
32. Walker, *Encyclopedia*, pp. 641–644.

## CHAPTER 8. THE GREAT MOTHER AS ARCHETYPAL DYNAMIC IN PERSONAL EXPERIENCE

1. Erich Neumann, *The Great Mother*, pp. 24–38.
2. Neumann, *GM*, p. 25.
3. Neumann, *GM*, pp. 39–46.
4. Neumann, *GM*, pp. 147–173.
5. Starhawk, *Dreaming the Dark*, p. 226.
6. Neumann, *GM*, pp. 24–38.
7. Neumann, *GM*, p. 59. See also pp. 284–286.
8. I am grateful to Sylvia Perera for pointing out this aspect of the transformative Mother to me in a personal communication.
9. See Perera, *Descent*, pp. 53–56.
10. Perera, *Descent*, pp. 30–42, pp. 59–62.
11. See Susan Faulkner's story in Karen Payne, *Between Ourselves*, pp. 357–359. Faulkner writes, "Dear Mother, A week ago you died and at last I am free—and quite alone. Free from that presence hovering perpetually in the wings I never stop looking to for the warmth and affection, the unreserved approval, that I knew only too well would never be there" (p. 358).
12. P. 53.
13. For a theory of feminine psychology rooted in the characteristics of both the "gestative" aspect of the womb and the "exertive," birth-giving womb, see Genia Pauli Haddon's highly original and provocative book, *Body Metaphors: Releasing God-Feminine in Us All* (New York: Crossroad Publishing Co., 1988).
14. Walker, *The Crone*, p. 86.
15. © Linda Daly Meshil, 1988.
16. Graves, *The Greek Myths, Vol. 1*, p. 93, n. 2.

## CHAPTER 9. ONE WOMAN'S JOURNEY

1. Toni Wolff, an early associate of Jung, developed a fourfold typology of women's "styles" of being feminine. In a paper entitled "Structural Forms of the Feminine Psyche" (Zurich: C. G. Jung Institute, 1956), she describes four feminine types: the mother, the hetaira, the amazon, and the medial woman. The medial woman is like our image of "psychic," a receptor for archetypal imagery and ideas. "The overwhelming force of the collective unconscious sweeps through the ego of the medial woman," Wolff writes (p. 9), and she is often overwhelmed and inarticulate. This was true of my patient at the beginning of therapy.
2. See Gimbutas, *Goddesses and Gods of Old Europe,* Fig. 15 (p. 46) and Fig. 96 (p. 144).

## CONCLUSION

1. Judy Grahn, *She Who* (Oakland, Calif.: Diana Press, 1972, 1977), pp. 8–9.

# BIBLIOGRAPHY

Andersen, Jorgen. *The Witch on the Wall.* Copenhagen: Rosenkilde and Bagger, 1977.

Arcana, Judith. *Our Mothers' Daughters.* Berkeley: Shameless Hussy Press, 1979.

Baumann, Carol. "Psychological Experiences Connected with Childbirth." *Studien zur Analytischen Psychologie C. G. Jungs,* vol. 1. Zurich: Rascher Verlag, 1955, pp. 336–370.

Bass, Ellen, and Davis, Laura. *The Courage to Heal: A Guide for Women Survivors of Child Sexual Abuse.* New York: Harper and Row, 1988.

Boer, Charles (transl.). *The Homeric Hymns.* Chicago: Swallow Press, 1970.

Brindel, June Rachuy. *Ariadne.* New York: St. Martin's Press, 1980.

Chodorow, Nancy. *The Reproduction of Mothering.* Berkeley and Los Angeles: University of California Press, 1978.

Christ, Carol. "Why Women Need the Goddess," in Carol Christ and Judith Plaskow (eds.), *Womanspirit Rising.* San Francisco: Harper and Row, 1979.

——— and Plaskow (eds.). *Womanspirit Rising.* San Francisco: Harper and Row, 1979.

Dames, Michael. *The Silbury Treasure.* London: Thames and Hudson, 1976.

de Castillejo, Irene. *Knowing Woman.* New York: C. G. Jung Foundation, 1973.

Dinnerstein, Dorothy. *The Mermaid and the Minotaur.* New York: Harper and Row, 1976.

Downing, Christine. *The Goddess.* New York: The Crossroad Publishing Co., 1981.

Fischer, Lucy Rose. *Linked Lives: Adult Daughters and Their Mothers.* New York: Harper and Row, 1986.

Flax, Jane. "The Conflict between Nurturance and Autonomy in Mother–Daughter Relationships and within Feminism." *Feminist Studies,* vol. 4, no. 2, June 1978, pp. 171–189.

Friday, Nancy. *My Mother, My Self.* New York: Delacorte Press, 1977.

Friederich, Paul. *The Meaning of Aphrodite.* Chicago and London: University of Chicago Press, 1978.

Gimbutas, Marija. *The Goddesses and Gods of Old Europe: Myths and Cult Images.* Berkeley and Los Angeles: University of California Press, 1982.

Grahn, Judy. *She Who.* Oakland, California: Diana Press, 1977.

Graves, Robert. *The Greek Myths,* Vol. 1. Middlesex, England: Penguin Books, 1955.

Greater Lansing Spinsters' Guild. *The Greengathering Feast* (songs). East Lansing, Michigan: Tea Rose Press, 1981.

Haddon, Genia Pauli. *Body Metaphors: Releasing God-Feminine in Us All.* New York: Crossroad Publishing Co., 1988.

Harding, Esther. *Women's Mysteries, Ancient and Modern.* London: Rider and Co., 1971.

Jung, Carl. "Psychological Aspects of the Mother Archetype," in *Collected Works, Vol. 9(i): The Archetypes and the Collective Unconscious.* Princeton: Princeton University Press, 1954, pp. 75–110.

———*Collected Works, Vol. 5: Symbols of Transformation.* Princeton: Princeton University Press, 1956.

Kinsley, David. *The Sword and the Flute: Kali and Krsna.* Berkeley and Los Angeles: University of California Press, 1975.

Lifshin, Lyn (ed.). *Tangled Vines: A Collection of Mother–Daughter Poems.* Boston: Beacon Press, 1978.

Miller, Jean Baker. *Toward a New Psychology of Women.* Boston: Beacon Press, 1976.

Neumann, Erich. *The Great Mother.* Princeton: Princeton University Press, 1955.

*New Larousse Encyclopedia of Mythology.* Middlesex, England: Hamlyn Publishing Group, 1959.

Nikhilananda, Swami. *The Gospel of Sri Ramakrishna by "M."* New York: Ramakrishna-Vivekananda Center, 1952.

Olsen, Tillie. *Tell Me a Riddle.* New York: Dell Publishing Co, 1960.

Ovid. *Metamorphoses.* Middlesex, England: Penguin Books, 1955.

Paris, Ginette. *Pagan Meditations: The Worlds of Aphrodite, Artemis, and Hestia.* Dallas: Spring Publications, 1986.

Payne, Karen (ed.). *Between Ourselves: Letters between Mothers and Daughters.* Boston: Houghton Mifflin Co., 1983.

Perera, Sylvia. *Descent to the Goddess*. Toronto: Inner City Books, 1981.

Piercy, Marge. *My Mother's Body*. New York: Alfred A. Knopf, 1985.

Preston, James. *Mother Worship*. Chapel Hill: University of North Carolina Press, 1982.

Rich, Adrienne. *The Dream of a Common Language*. New York: W. W. Norton and Co., 1978.

———*Of Woman Born*. New York: W. W. Norton and Co., 1976.

Sexton, Anne. *The Complete Poems*. Boston: Houghton Mifflin, 1981.

Sjöö, Monica and Mor, Barbara. *The Great Cosmic Mother*. San Francisco: Harper and Row, 1987.

Spretnak, Charlene (ed.). *The Politics of Women's Spirituality*. Garden City, New York: Anchor Press, 1982.

Shuttle, Penelope and Redgrove, Peter. *The Wise Wound: Eve's Curse and Everywoman*. New York: Richard Marek Publishers, 1978.

Starhawk. *Dreaming the Dark*. Boston: Beacon Press, 1982.

———*The Spiral Dance*. San Francisco: Harper and Row, 1979.

Steinem, Gloria. *Outrageous Acts and Everyday Rebellions*. New York: Holt, Rhinehart, and Winston, 1983.

Stone, Merlin. *When God Was a Woman*. New York and London: Harcourt Brace Jovanovich, 1976.

Ulanov, Ann. "The Witch Archetype." *Quadrant* (Journal of the C. G. Jung Foundation, New York City), Vol. 10, No. 1, Summer 1977, pp. 5–22.

Walker, Barbara. *The Crone*. San Francisco: Harper and Row, 1985.

———*The Women's Encyclopedia of Myths and Secrets*. San Francisco: Harper and Row, 1983.

Warner, Marina. *Alone of All Her Sex: The Myth and Cult of the Virgin Mary*. New York: Alfred A. Knopf, 1976.

Wolff, Toni. "Structural Forms of the Feminine Psyche." Zurich: C. G. Jung Institute, 1956.

Wolkstein, Diane and Kramer, Samuel Noah. *Inanna, Queen of Heaven and Earth*. New York: Harper and Row, 1983.

# INDEX


Aging, 75, 78, 83
Apple trees, 130
Arcana, Judith, 19
Archetypal mother, 9–10, 65, 73, 86–87, 102, 112, 126
  bi-valent, 9, 83, 89, 93, 139n.20
*Ariadne* (Brindel), 74
Autonomy, 24, 25, 99, 135n.2
  taboo on, 29, 32

Banishing mother, 24, 25, 33–35
  filial competence and, 33–34
  negative transformative Mother and, 101
*Between Ourselves* (Payne), 24
Binding mother(s), 24–33, 114, 120
  approval/disapproval, 25–28
  negative elementary Mother and, 97–98
Birth-death-rebirth cycle, 72, 83–84, 128.
  *See also* Triple Goddess
Birthing, 72, 75, 78, 89
  symbolic, 105–106, 140n.13
Bi-valent Great Mother, 9, 83, 89, 93, 139n.20
  as process, 83
Body image, 38, 42–43, 48
Body therapy, 42–43, 128
Breasts (Goddess's), 79, fig. 3

Catholic Church, 76
Child-rearing (patriarchal), 3, 133n.1
Child's view of mother, xiii, 1–4, 7, 11, 54, 65
  limitations of, 4
Choice-making, 25–26, 31–32, 35, 135n.6
Christ, Carol, 77
Christianity, 76, 77
Claes, Helen, 24
Competitiveness/envy (maternal), 29–31
"Container" (maternal), 21, 22, 44, 45, 88, 94, 97
  consistency and, 21
Corrective experience, 34, 35–36
"Counter-mothers," 6, 117, 126
Crone, 83–84, 87, 111
  Black, and crow, 109

Daughter(s), 71, 85–86, 94, 111–113
  achievements of, 28, 29–31, 100
  "anything-but-mother," 51
  spiritual quest of, 73
*Daughters and Mothers, Mothers and Daughters* (Hammer), 27, 28–29
Death, 83, 84–85
  Egyptian sarcophagi, 84, fig. 16
Demeter (Goddess), 86, 99
  and Kore, 86, 94
Denial, 7, 62, 67
Dependency dynamics, 35, 67
  and patriarchal child-rearing, 3
Dreaming forth Goddess, 75, 89–92
Dreams/visions, 77, 95–96, 103–109, 112, 113, 120, 123–124, 129–132

Eastman, Annis, 15–16
Eastman, Crystal, 15–16, 95
"Elementary" Mother, 93–99, 103
  manifestations of, 94–97
  negative, 97–98, 102, 103
  positive, 94–97, 98
  symbolism of, 94

"The Envelope" (Kumin), 49
Eyes (Goddess's), 79, 85, fig. 4
Experiencing Goddess (Great Mother), 10–11, 87, 139n.29

Fairy godmother, 99
"False" self, 51
Fantasy, 112, 128–129
Father(s), 20, 22, 134nn.6,7
Female body, 38, 48, 72, 117–118, 122, 123
  "armoring," 41
  cultural images of, 38, 40, 42
  fat and, 117–118
  Great Goddess and, 77, 78
  hatred of, 41–42
Female power, 75, 77, 89, 90
Feminine, the, 77, 117
  as deity, 9. *See also* Goddess
  remythologizing, 106
"Feminine arts." *See* Transformational activities
Feminine creativity, 90–91, 105
  introversion and, 90–91
  menstrual blood as symbol of, 90–91
Feminine experience, 72, 75, 78, 79, 88, 89
  reclaiming significance of, 88
  sacredness of, 72, 75, 88
  transpersonal, 10–11, 72–73, 77, 85–87, 89, 139n.29
Feminine heritage, 10, 77
Feminine wisdom, 78, 85
Feminist view of mother, xiii, 1, 5–8, 11
  limitation of, 6–8
  Friday, Nancy, 19

Genitals (Goddess's), 80, figs. 5, 6, 7
God. *See* Goddess
Goddess, 9, 66, 74–92
  Catholic Church and, 76
  as creatrix, 72, 74, 75, 79, 82, 87
  as destroyer, 83–85, 87–88
  as huntress, 88
  images/stories of, 10–11, 88, 89–92, 112, 114
  as law, 88
  patriarchal invaders and, 75–76, 86
  religion of, 75–76, 86, 137n.2
  sexuality and, 79–80
Goddess (body), 78, 85, 123, fig. 4
  breasts, 79, fig. 3
  eyes, 79, 85, fig. 4
  genitals, 80, figs. 5, 6, 7
  womb, 72, 79, fig. 2
Goddess (Great Mother), 9–11, 74, 82–92, 123–125, figs. 11, 12,
  as Child-Eater, 97
  creation myths of, 78
  as gorgon, 83, 97
  as symbol, 82
  as vulture, 83, fig. 15
Goddess (as Nature), 81, 90, 102
  attributes of, 81
  bird companions of, 81, fig. 10
  expressions of, 81, fig. 9
  as "mermaid," 81, 114
  moon symbol of, 81
Goddess (Triple), 83–84, 111
  crone, 83–84, 87, 109, 111
  maiden, 83, 84, 87, 111
  mother, 83, 87, 111
God image
  feminine, 3, 10, 74, 75, 76
  masculine, 3, 76, 125
"Good Mother," 9, 94, 131
*The Great Mother* (Neumann), 82
Great Mother/personal experience, 93, 113
  elementary aspect of, 93–99, 102, 103
  transformative aspect of, 93, 98–102, 109
Grief work, 68

Hades (Lord of the Underworld), 86
Hammer, Signe, 27
Happiness, 31

Healing, 10, 112–113
  anger (rage) and, 4, 119, 133n.5
  *See also* Transformation
Hinduism, 76
"Homeric Hymn to Demeter," 86, 139n.26
Homophobia, 44, 46, 47

Identity, sense of, 32, 54
  maternal, 23, 27–29
Images/visions
  of Goddess, 10–11, 75, 88, 89–92, 112, 114
  of inner/outer mother, 37, 60, 128
  traditional, of women, 5, 32–33, 35, 75
Inanna (Goddess), 80
Inner child, 68–70, 102–103, 106. *See also* Unhealed child
Inner male, 125
Inner mother, 50, 52–55, 57–60, 126, 128
  as "shadow," 55
  transformation of, 55, 57–60
Inner security, 14–15, 32, 40
  touch and, 40
Insecurity (maternal), 31
Instincts (maternal), 5
Intimacy, 20, 34, 48
Introjected mother. *See* Inner mother

Journal writing, xiii, 39, 58
Judaism, 76, 77
Jung, Carl, 51, 117, 136n.3

Kali (Goddess), 85, 108–109, fig. 17
Kore (Goddess), 83, 86, 94, 111
Kumin, Maxine, 49

Legitimate needs, 58, 61
"Lost" mother, 19–20, 86–87

Maiden, 83, 84, 87, 88, 111
Male
  deity, 3, 76, 125
  inner, 125
Maternal
  competitiveness/envy, 29–31
  deprivation, 101–102, 140n.11
  insecurity, 31
  instincts, 5
  resentment, 2
  violence, 39, 40, 135n.1
Maternal "container," 21, 22, 44, 45, 88, 94, 97
  consistency and, 21
Maternal touch, 39–40
  patriarchal thinking and, 47, 136n.4. *See also* Touch
Matrophobia, 49–60
  archetypal perspective, 97–98
  definition of, 49
  "false self," and, 51
  magical thinking and, 54
  transformation of, 49, 55, 57–60
"Medial woman," 115, 140n.1
Meditation, 58, 87, 112
Menopause, 75, 78, 138n.11
Menstrual blood, 72, 78, 138nn.9,10
  myths of, 89–91
  withholding, and feminine creativity, 90–91
Menstrual taboos, 90
Menstruation, 72, 75
Merging vs. bonding, 26–29, 116, 118–119, 120
Mermaid, 81, 114
Moon symbol, 81
Mother(s), xi–xii, 19, 83, 87, 88, 111
  access to, 11
  archetypal, 9–10, 65, 73, 86–87
  inner, 19, 50, 52–53, 54–55
  "lost," 19–20, 86–87
  negative power of, 54
  outer, 54–55
  revisioning, 9, 73
  as role model, 21, 34, 56, 73
  spiritual context, 72–73
  stereotypes, 3, 4, 9, 35
  as windows to Great Mother, 93
Mother(s): three perspectives
  child's view, xiii, 1–4, 11

feminist view, xiii, 1, 5–8, 11
transpersonal view, xiii, 1, 8–11
Mother-daughter relationship, xi–xiii, 2, 69, 109–111
autonomy and, 24
choice-making and, 25–26, 31–32, 35, 135n.6
fathers and, 20, 22, 134nn.6,7
intimacy and, 20, 34, 48
maternal self-esteem and, 21
nurturance and, 4, 21, 24, 34, 135n.2
socialization process and, 5, 133n.3
spiritual context of, 77, 85–87
touch and, 38–48
"Mother Nature," 81, fig. 8. *See also* Goddess (as Nature)
Motherhood, institution of, 5, 133n.2
Mothering, 75
Myths of the feminine, 74, 85–86, 89–91
new, 89–92
old, 89–92

Naming ourselves, 75
Neumann, Erich, 82
Nurturance, 4, 21, 24, 34, 96, 99
autonomy and, 24, 99, 135n.2

*Of Woman Born* (Rich), 49
Old Religion, 78, 79, 81, 83, 84, 122, 128
Outer (personal) mother, 54–55, 57–60, 65–66, 127, 128

Pantheism, 81
Patriarchal
child-rearing, 3, 133n.1
invasions, 75–76, 86
religions, 76
taboos, 91
Payne, Karen, 24
Persephone (Goddess), 111
Positive bonds, 12–23, 24, 94
fathers and, 20, 22, 134nn.6,7
interference with, 22–23, 86, 134n.5
mutual attachment and, 20
protectiveness and, 21–22
psychic imprint of, 15, 17
separation/autonomy and, 15, 23, 26, 99
Power
experience of "positive," 75, 89
myths of Blood, 89–91
"negative," of mother, 54
Pregnancy, 72, 78, 89
symbolic, 105, 140n.13
Prepatriarchal religion(s), 9. *See also* Old Religion
Priestesses, persecution of, 76, 137n.3
Psychic imprints
negative, 35, 40
positive, 15, 17, 40

Ramakrishna, 85
Regression, 45, 67, 135n.3
Relationship(s)
mother-daughter, xi–xiii, 1–10, 21, 24, 38–48, 77, 85–87, 109–111, 126
with men, 67, 136n.2
with women, 6, 70, 117, 126
Religions
Goddess, 75–76, 86, 137n.2
patriarchal, 76
Rich, Adrienne, 49, 61, 71, 89, 136n.1

Sekhmet (Goddess), 84, Fig. 15
Selective approval/disapproval, 28
binding mothers and, 25, 28
Self-assertion, 4, 100
Self-interest, 4, 29, 32
Self-worth, 4, 7, 116
Separation, 4, 15, 23, 25–26, 86–87, 118, 126
positive bonding and, 15, 23, 26, 99
Sexton, Anne, 14–15, 26–27
Sexuality, 48, 72, 75, 116–117, 123
Goddess and, 79
spirituality and, 88

Shadow, the, 55
"She Who," 131–132
Spock, Dr. Benjamin, 5–6
Stone, Merlin, 79, 122

Therapy, 34, 36, 46–47, 52, 57, 58–59, 95, 104–105
  body-, 42–43, 128
  dreams and, 77, 95–96, 104–109, 112, 113, 120, 123–124
  Goddess and, 77, 137n.7
"Three Generations" (Meshill), 110–111
Touch
  "Going dead" and, 41–42
  homophobia and, 46
  hunger, 43–45
  inhibition of, 48, 136n.4
  invasive, 39–40, 41
  phobia, 44, 45
  sexualized, 43, 46
  as "truth" of body, 39
Touch hunger/touch phobia, 43–48
  regression and, 45, 135n.3
Transformation, 49, 55, 57–60, 98–102
Transformative activities, 99–100
"Transformative" Mother, 93, 98–102
  manifestations of, 99, 100
  negative, 100–102, 109
  positive, 99–100
Transpersonal view of mother, xiii, 1, 8–11
Triple Goddess. *See* Goddess (Triple)

Unhealed child, xii, 3–4, 7, 34, 55–56, 61–73, 102–103, 112–113
  compensatory experiences and, 102–103
  denial of, 7, 62, 67
  feminist views and, 6–7, 134n.6
  grief work and, 68
  political passion and, 71–72
  rage (anger), 4, 61, 62, 72, 119, 133n.5
  relationships with men and, 67, 136n.2
  spiritual dimensions of, 72–73
  yearnings of, 61–62

Violence (maternal), 39, 40, 135n.1
Virgin Mary, 76, 137n.5

*When God Was A Woman* (Stone), 79, 122
Wicked stepmother, 100
Wolff, Toni, 115
Womb, 72, 79, fig. 2
  transpersonal meaning, 106
Women
  devaluation of, 4, 75
  individuation task of, 10, 75
  older, 78
  supportive relationships with, 6, 70, 117, 126
  traditional images of, 5, 32–33, 35, 75
Women's Movement, 33, 35, 70
Women's spirituality, xii, 76–77, 137n.6
  Movement, 77

Zeus (God), 76, 86

# CREDITS

The author would like to thank the following publishers for permission to reprint material copyrighted or controlled by them: Beacon Press for permission to quote from the chant "She changes everything she touches" from *Dreaming the Dark: Magic, Sex, and Politics* by Starhawk, copyright © 1982, 1988 by Miriam Simos; reprinted by permission of Beacon Press; The Crossing Press for permission to quote "She Who Continues" from *Work of a Common Woman* by Judy Grahn, copyright © 1978 by Judy Grahn, published by The Crossing Press, 1985; Harper and Row and Diane Wolkstein for excerpts from *Inanna: Queen of Heaven and Earth,* by Diane Wolkstein and Samuel Noah Kramer, copyright © 1983 by Diane Wolkstein and Samuel Noah Kramer, reprinted by permission of Harper and Row, Publishers, Inc., and Diane Wolkstein; Houghton Mifflin Company for excerpts from "7" of "The Double Image" from *To Bedlam and Part Way Back* by Anne Sexton, copyright © 1960 by Anne Sexton, reprinted by permission of Houghton Mifflin Company; Houghton Mifflin Company and Sterling Lord Literistic, Inc., for permission to quote "Mothers" from *The Awful Rowing Toward God* by Anne Sexton, copyright © 1975 by Loring Conant, Jr., Executor of the Estate of Anne Sexton, reprinted by permission of Houghton Mifflin Company and Sterling Lord Literistic, Inc.; Princeton University Press and Routledge Publishers for permission to quote "Song of the Kagaba Indians, Colombia" from Erich Neumann, *The Great Mother: An Analysis of the Archetype,* trans. Ralph Mannheim, Bollingen Series 47, copyright, 1955, © 1980 renewed by Princeton University Press, reprinted with permission of Princeton University Press and Routledge Publishers; Viking Penguin, Inc., for permission to quote "The Envelope" from *Our Ground Time Here Will Be Brief* by Maxine Kumin, copyright © 1978 by Maxine Kumin. All rights reserved. Reprinted by permission of Viking Penguin, a division of Penguin Books USA, Inc. Every endeavor has been made to contact copyright holders.

# Other C.G. Jung Foundation Books from Shambhala Publications

ROBERT H. HOPCKE

A Guided Tour of the Collected Works of C.G. Jung

JEROME S. BERNSTEIN

Power and Politics

The Psychology of Soviet-American Partnership

Forewords by Senator Claiborne Pell and Edward C. Whitmont, M.D.

STEPHEN SEGALLER and MERRILL BERGER

The Wisdom of the Dream

The World of C.G. Jung